HOW TO PRAY

FOR THE RELEASE OF THE HOLY SPIRIT

Also by Dennis Bennett:
   Nine O'Clock in the Morning

With Rita Bennett:
   The Holy Spirit and You
   The Holy Spirit and You Supplement

HOW TO PRAY

FOR THE RELEASE OF THE HOLY SPIRIT

What The Baptism Of The Holy Spirit Is & How To Pray For It

Dennis Bennett

Bridge-Logos *Publishers*

Gainesville, Florida 32614 USA

All scripture quotations are from the King James Version of
the Bible unless otherwise noted.

How To Pray for the Release of the Holy Spirit
by Dennis Bennett
International Standard Book Number: 0-88270-593-8
Library of Congress Catalog Card Number: 85-72459
Copyright © 1985 by Bridge-Logos Publishers
Reprinted 2001

Published by:
Bridge-Logos *Publishers*
Gainesville, Florida FL 32614, USA
http://www.bridgelogos.com

CONTENTS

INTRODUCTION

God is exciting and wonderful, and knowing Him is what life is all about. In spite of this, for many people, even if they've accepted Jesus, Christianity is not exciting at all. This is because, although the Spirit of God may be living in them, He's still locked up inside. He needs to be set free so they can become more aware of Him and enjoy Him, and so God can work strongly through them to do the things He wants to do.

In the first two chapters of Acts, you can read how much the first friends of Jesus changed after the Spirit was set free in them. That can happen to you, too. You can have the same kind of power, love, and joy those first Christians had. You can be just as aware of God as they were. You can experience freely the gifts and fruit of the Holy Spirit. God can use you to help other people supernaturally, by wisdom and knowledge, healings, and miracles, and this will show them God is real.

Because so many people in the historic churches have been baptized in the Holy Spirit over the past thirty-five years and more, a great renewal has been moving throughout the world. Let us not forget that this renewal is rooted in a release of the Holy Spirit, and will only continue as people continue to receive this release and walk in the freedom of the Spirit.

After you have received Jesus and the baptism in the Holy Spirit, suppose that each day you tell two others, leading them also to receive the Lord and the release of the Spirit. Further suppose that each of them daily reaches two others in the same way, and each of them two more, and so forth. In just a month and a day the whole world would have been reached!

This is how Jesus expected the good news to spread, but it won't happen unless people are baptized or released in the Holy Spirit, so it's vital that you be free yourself, and that you know how to help others.

NOBODY IN THE NEW TESTAMENT FAILED TO RECEIVE THE
BAPTISM IN THE HOLY SPIRIT

In New Testament times nobody failed to receive
the baptism in the Spirit when they asked for it, and
there's no reason for you to fail when you ask, or when
you ask for other people. I've often seen twenty, thirty,
or even a hundred receive all at once, just as they did
on the day of Pentecost, and there's no reason why this
shouldn't happen with you if you get people to
understand what they are looking for, and prepare them
properly.

A HANDBOOK

This is an on-the-job handbook. Ever since I was
baptized in the Spirit in 1959, a sizable part of my life
has been spent teaching and praying with people about
it. For twenty-one years I was pastor of St. Luke's
Episcopal Church in Seattle, the first "historic" church
to urge people openly to receive the freedom of the
Spirit. I estimate that over the last twenty-five years
(as of 1985), I've prepared and prayed with at least
25,000 people. I have tried to show through this book
just how to go about it. I hope it will help you, and
help others through you.

It's Important to Prepare People

Folks find it hard to receive the release of the Spirit because they don't know exactly what it is, and what is supposed to happen to them, so don't give way to the temptation to pray with people without preparing them. Don't be influenced by the hopeful crowd who are standing at the front of the auditorium waiting for you to lay hands on them! Don't be pressured by the sight of a couple of dozen people kneeling at the altar ready to *wrestle* with the Lord to give them the Holy Spirit!

If you just lay hands on these folks without preparing them, many will go home frustrated, feeling there must be something wrong with them, because they think God has refused them; and perhaps for the third or fourth time, or more. Some people have been *tarrying* for the Holy Spirit for twenty and thirty years, and there are many, even in the historic Pentecostal churches, who have not received, and often have just about despaired of receiving. Unfortunately, this leads people to think that perhaps the baptism in the Spirit is not for everybody. Don't help propagate this wrong idea by praying without preparing.

First Timothy 5:22 tells us not to lay hands *suddenly* on anybody. This may refer primarily to ordaining elders, but it certainly also applies to the baptism with the Holy Spirit. Some people come seeking the Holy Spirit when they don't yet know Jesus. Others need to renounce wrong beliefs and attitudes they've had. If they are prayed for without preparation they can get into real confusion, so don't begrudge the time you spend working with them.

If you prepare people well, most will receive easily. So tell the seekers you want to talk to them, and invite them to sit down, relax, and listen.

It's Important to Prepare Yourself

It goes without saying that the more you prepare yourself, the more effective you will be in helping other people. You should know the Scriptures, and especially those that concern the work of the Spirit. You should have read other books on the topic.

Especially you need to read *The Holy Spirit and You* (Bridge-Logos Publishers) carefully. It tells in detail what the baptism with the Holy Spirit is, how to prepare to receive it, and how to receive it. It tells what the gifts and fruit of the Spirit are, and how we experience them. Although my wife, Rita, and I completed *The Holy Spirit and You* in 1971, I don't know of another book that covers the subject as thoroughly.

I also recommend that you read *Trinity of Man,* which explains the three areas of our beings: spirit, soul, and body; how they are interrelated, and how each part can be healed through Jesus. It will show you in story and diagram what salvation is, and what the baptism with the Holy Spirit is. This easy-to-read book will help you a great deal in teaching others.

BAPTISM OR RELEASE

You'll notice in the title of this book, and occasionally in the book itself, I use the term "release of the Holy Spirit" in the place of "baptism in the Holy Spirit."

This isn't because I think there's anything wrong with calling the Pentecost experience "the baptism in the Holy Spirit." After all, that's what Jesus Himself called it in Acts 1:5, and the phrase is used by God the Father Himself (John 1:33); John the Baptist (Matthew 3:11; Mark 1:8; Luke 3:16); Peter (Acts 11:16) and many other New Testament writers. The term often raises hackles though, because some believers think we're saying that those who have accepted Jesus as Savior still need to *get* the Holy Spirit. I want to make it clear I believe the Holy Spirit is already living in every Christian, but that many need to *accept* that He is in them and release Him so He can give them the fullness of His love and power.

Also, "baptism in the Spirit" can trouble people from the sacramental traditions, such as Lutherans, Episcopalians, Roman Catholics, and Eastern Orthodox, and also such groups as the Church of Christ, because these all lay great emphasis on the outward rite of water baptism, and they cannot understand why people are being urged to seek *another* baptism. (I talk about this, and the meaning of the word *baptism*, in Chapter One.) I don't want to turn people off before they read this book; I want them to find out what I am actually saying; that's why I used the expression "release of the Spirit" in the title.

As a matter of fact, there are a number of names we might use for what the New Testament often calls being baptized *with* or *in* the Holy Spirit. (The Greek preposition used in the New Testament *is en,* which can mean either "in" or "with.") You may speak of the release of the Spirit, the overflowing of the Spirit, being overwhelmed by the Spirit, being empowered by the Spirit, and so forth. By the way, I do not think it is good to use the term "Spirit-filled" to mean that someone has been baptized in the Holy Spirit. Many people are *filled* with the Spirit without being *baptized* in the Spirit. Long before Pentecost we read of people being filled with the Holy Spirit. John the Baptist is one example of this, as are many of the Old Testament people. The baptism in the Spirit is not the *infilling,* but the *outpouring* of the Spirit. If you have a problem with this, please read Chapter One carefully on the meaning of *baptism.*

THE FORMAT OF THIS BOOK

Most of the time I am giving here what I would typically say when instructing a group, so much of the time I'm writing as if I were talking to the people. You don't have to use my exact words, of course, but they will give you a pattern to follow. Familiarize yourself with them, and then let the Lord guide you. There's probably a lot more material here than you will use at any one time, because I have tried to cover all the bases. Get to know it, though, and then let the Holy Spirit lead you concerning what and how much to use.

You may want to use this book for a series of teaching sessions, and in that case you will be able to use more of the material and go into more detail.

From time to time I will be talking directly to you. The parts where I am speaking to you (when they are not in a separate section or chapter) will be set off in brackets: [   ].

IF YOU ARE PRAYING FOR YOURSELF

If you are praying for yourself to receive, simply do privately what I am suggesting to the group.

USING THIS BOOK AS A TEACHING SERIES

You may want to use this book as the basis for a weekly series of classes. For this purpose the teaching could be divided into five sessions, as follows:

1. "What the Baptism in the Holy Spirit Is." Chapters 1 and 2. The triune person.

2. "Speaking in Tongues." Chapter 3. What speaking in tongues is, and why it is important.

3. "How to Prepare." Chapters 4 and 5. Receiving Jesus, and the forgiveness of sins, and letting God deal with wrong attitudes. Renouncing involvement with cults and the occult.

4. "How to Receive the Baptism in the Holy Spirit." Chapters 6, 7, 8 and 9. Prayer for receiving the baptism in the Holy Spirit.

5. "What Next?" A follow-up session to help people continue their life in the Spirit

You could, of course, make a different division of topics, and increase or decrease the number of weeks.

If you follow this plan, it would be a good idea to have the people read *The Holy Spirit and You* as home study during the period of the classes. You could also use the *Holy Spirit and You Supplement.*

SCRIPTURE REFERENCES

Unless otherwise noted, quotations are from the King James Version of the Bible. Reference notations are:

TLB, The Living Bible
RSV, Revised Standard Version
JB, Jerusalem Bible
LG, Literal Greek
AP, author's paraphrase from the Greek
BE, Basic English Version

1

WHAT THE BAPTISM WITH THE HOLY SPIRIT IS

Perhaps you have only just heard about the baptism with the Holy Spirit, or you may have asked for it before, perhaps many times, and have been discouraged because nothing seemed to happen—yet you really didn't know what was *supposed* to happen. The more you understand what you're looking for, the more easily you will find it.

The word "baptism" itself may confuse you. It usually is used to mean the ceremony of baptism with water, in which people are dipped in water, or water is sprinkled or poured on them as a sign they have received Jesus, their sins have been washed away, and they have joined the family of God. The phrase

1

"baptism with the Holy Spirit," however, uses the word in a broader sense.

WHAT "BAPTISM" MEANS

The word "baptize" comes from the Greek *baptizo* (pronounced bapp-teedzo), which means to overcome or *overwhelm* something or someone. In classical Greek, a sunken ship, lying on the bottom of the ocean, drenched or overwhelmed by the water-waterlogged-was said to be "baptized."

A person is "baptized," then, when he is completely overwhelmed by, or identified with, something or someone else. Paul uses the word this way in First Corinthians 10:2 when he says the children of Israel were all "baptized into Moses," by which he means they made a complete "commitment to Moses as their leader," as *The Living Bible* puts it.

You are spirit, soul and body. Your soul is the psychological part of you, and your body is the physical part. Your spirit is the part that is *like* God (in His image), so that you can relate to Him on a person-to-Person basis. However, because the human race rejected God from the very beginning, your spirit was born separated from God, and so, as Jesus said, needed to be "born from above" (John 3:3 LG)—it needed to come alive to God.

This happens when you receive Jesus into your life. When you accept Him, then your sins and everything that separated you from God and your fellow humans are taken away, and God comes to live in you. God's Spirit joins Himself to your spirit, and you become a "new creation." The Spirit of God totally overwhelms or baptizes your spirit. Paul says, "He that is joined unto the Lord is one spirit" (1 Corinthians 6:17).

This is the most important thing that can ever happen to you. This is the basic baptism, of which baptism with water is the normal outward sign.

A friend of ours wrote this little verse,

Put a little sugar into your tea,
That's what Jesus did when He put Himself in me.
Now you can't take the sugar out of the tea
And you can't take Jesus out of me!

WHY *ANOTHER* BAPTISM?

Folks say, "Okay, I'm baptized into Christ, why do I need *another* baptism? Paul says there's 'one Lord, one faith, one baptism'" (Ephesians 4:5).

But Jesus talked about a second baptism. He said, "John baptized with water, but you shall be baptized in the Holy Spirit in just a few days" (Acts 1:5, RSV).

Really there is just one baptism, and that's the one we've just been talking about, the inner baptism that takes place when we receive Jesus, when the Holy Spirit brings us alive in Christ and God comes to live in us. This is what makes everything else possible. Different kinds of Christians use different names for this essential first experience. Some would call it being born again, some would speak of regeneration, which is a fancy word for "born again". Others would talk of being saved, or redeemed, or converted.

But there are two parts to this one baptism. In the first part, the Holy Spirit comes to live in you. In the second half He begins to move out from within your spirit to flood, overwhelm, drench, soak, overcome the rest of your being, that is, your soul and body, and then move out through you to the world around you. This part is the baptism with the Holy Spirit.

When Jesus talked to the woman at the well in Samaria He said, "If you knew Who was asking you for a drink of water, you would have asked Him to give you a drink. And after drinking the water I gave you, you'd never be thirsty again!" But then He added, "The water that I'd give you would be a fountain of water in you, springing up into ever-renewed [eternal or ageless] life!" (John 4:14, AP).

On another occasion Jesus said, "If anybody is thirsty, let him come to Me and drink." But again, He didn't stop with this. He went on, "If anyone really trusts Me, rivers of living water will flow out of his

4

belly!" The next verse explains, "In this He was speaking of the Spirit, which those who believed in Him would receive, for the Holy Spirit was not yet given, because Jesus was not yet glorified" (John 7:37-39, AP).

INFLOW AND OUTFLOW: THE *RELEASE* OF THE SPIRIT

Do you see that both of these times Jesus was first talking about an *in*flow of the Spirit, and then an *out*flow of the Spirit? The *inflow* is salvation, the first half of baptism, the *outflow* is the baptism with the Holy Spirit, the second half of baptism. In the first half, when you receive Jesus, the Holy Spirit comes *in:* baptizes, soaks, drenches, overwhelms your spirit, and brings it to new life.

The second half of baptism is when the Holy Spirit, living in your spirit, flows *out* to baptize, soak, drench, overwhelm your soul (psychological nature, including your emotions, will, intellect, subconscious) and your body, and bring them to new life, freedom, joy and peace in and through the Lord Jesus. Then He can flow out into the world from you to bring love, peace, joy, and healing to other people.

So you see you aren't trying to get the Holy Spirit to come *in* to you. You aren't trying to get God to send you Someone or something you don't already have. People spend years struggling to receive the baptism with the Holy Spirit because they are trying to get God to send the Spirit to them from Heaven. But if you've accepted Jesus, God Himself cannot give you the Holy Spirit, for the simple reason that He already has *given* Him to you! He gave Him to you when you asked Jesus into your life! (John 1:12-13; Acts 2:38). Jesus said, "If anyone loves me he will keep my word, and my Father will love him, and we shall come to him and make our home with him" (John 14:23b, JB}. Then He said, "I will ask the Father, and He will give you another Helper [the Holy Spirit] to be with you always" (John 14:16, LG).

According to these Scriptures, if you have received Jesus, then the Father, Son, and Holy Spirit are all living in you, so rather obviously you can't be expecting anyone else to come from Heaven! They've all come! Don't be discouraged then, or think there's something wrong with you and that God is refusing to give you the Holy Spirit. What is needed is not an *incoming*, but an *outflowing* of the Spirit.

NOT A REWARD FOR HOLINESS

One stanza of a popular chorus says,

My Lord and I, we got so close,
He baptized me in the Holy Ghost.

It's a fun song, but it reflects the popular idea that in order to *get* the baptism in the Spirit, you must make yourself a *fit vessel* for God to come and live in. Maybe

6

you were taught that the baptism with the Holy Spirit is a reward for being good, a sign of special holiness, and that you've got to make yourself holy before you can expect the Holy Spirit to come to you. But since the Spirit Himself is the only One who can make you holy, to say you must be holy in order to receive the baptism with the Holy Spirit is like saying you must be educated before you may go to school, or clean before you may take a bath! If only clean people were allowed to bathe, everyone would be very dirty!

To be *holy is* to be *whole,* or *healthy.* These three words are from the same root. *Holy* means to be more like Jesus, Who is perfectly whole and healthy. The Holy Spirit wants to make you holy, and He's going to do it from where He's already living inside you. When He came into your spirit, He made it perfectly healthy and holy. If you've accepted Jesus, your spirit is already in fellowship with God, and so it must be holy, otherwise God couldn't live there. When Paul says you *are* sitting together in heavenly places in Christ Jesus (Ephesians 2:6), He is talking about your spirit. Your emotions may not feel that way right now, but your spirit is aware of God all the time. The problem is that you are not aware of your *spirit* all the time! That's because you are in the habit of living from your soul—intellect, will, and emotions—and trusting these to guide you. Then, too, your soul has been hurt, so it demands attention. As it gets healed, you will find it easier to respond to your spirit—and to the Holy Spirit Who is living in your spirit.

[Don't go any further until you are sure the people understand that if they have received Jesus, the Holy Spirit is already living in them. Be sure they see they are not praying to get the Holy Spirit into them, but are trying to release Him so He can flow out.]

2

YOU FIRST!

THE HOLY SPIRIT IS A PERSONAL BEING

The Holy Spirit is not like "the Force" in Star Wars. And you shouldn't think or speak of Him as if He were like gasoline or electricity. Try not to say things like, "I want to get more of the Holy Spirit." The Holy Spirit is a Person, so you can't have little or much of Him. He doesn't come in increments.

If I said, "I hear John Jackson is at your house," and you replied, "Well, some of him is. Part of him arrived yesterday, more of him is coming tomorrow, and we're hoping to get the rest of him next week," I would think your friend John was in pretty bad shape. We don't talk about people like that, because people are *personal* beings, not impersonal substances or forces. You can talk about forces or substances in terms of quantity—you can talk about a gallon of gasoline, or a kilowatt-hour of electricity—but if a human person is at your house, all of him is there (unless he or she is standing halfway in the front door.).

It's the same with the Holy Spirit. He is a Person too, that is to say He can say "I." He's not a human being, of course, but a divine Person. So you shouldn't say, "I have some of the Holy Spirit, and I'm looking for more." If God has given you His Spirit, He has given Him, and all of Him is living in you.

On the other hand, let's say your friend John is at your house, and you have left him sitting in the living room. You don't want to let him into the kitchen because you haven't done the dishes. You don't want him in the bedroom, because the beds aren't made, and you certainly don't want him in the rumpus room, because the kids tore that up last night. So even though it doesn't make sense to ask, "How much of John do you have in your house," it does make sense to inquire, "How much of your house is John in?" That is, "How much of your house does he have access to?" In the same way, though it's not right to ask, "How much of the Holy Spirit do you have?" it is valid to ask, "How much of you does the Holy Spirit have? How much of your life's house have you let Him into?"

Some years ago, my older son said, "You know, I had a funny dream last night. I dreamed I had God locked up in the closet in my bedroom, and He was

10

shouting through the door, 'When are you going to let Me out of here? "

Being baptized in the Spirit isn't getting God to come in. You need to let Him out into the rest of your house—into your soul and body. You need to tell Him, "The place is yours. Make yourself at home."

When you let the Spirit of God out into your soul (the psychological part of you) He baptizes your intellect (thoughts), your emotions (feelings), and your will (motivations and desires). When you let Him into your body (the physical part of you), He gives you health and strength, yes, and keeps you young, too. All this is not just theory. It really happens. After you're baptized in the Holy Spirit you'll find yourself thinking in a new way, feeling in a new way, and really wanting to do what God wants you to with a new, joyful eagerness. And you'll be likely to find an increase in your stamina, too—a new sense of physical well-being.

You may sometimes feel Him present in your body by pleasant physical sensations. Enjoy these feelings if and when they come, but don't depend on them. Be very careful about using physical feelings for discernment. The gift of discernment, like other spiritual gifts, comes from your spirit. It may touch your soul and body, and bring physical feelings, but be very wary of using these physical feelings themselves as signs that something is true or false, or that someone's teaching is right. Above all, never wait for feelings before you begin to do what you know God wants you to do. He can work through you no matter how you feel.

YOU FIRST!

Notice that when you do let God flow out from your spirit into your soul and body, you get blessed first. You probably have been taught that everyone else is supposed to get good things from God first, and then if there's anything left, you get some. It may surprise you to realize the scriptural order is that God blesses you first, then blesses others through you.

That's what He told Abraham back in the beginning. He said, "I'm going to bless you, and I'm going to make you a blessing, and through your seed I'm going to bless all the families of the earth." (See Genesis 12:2-3, 22:17-18; 26:3-4; 28:13-14.) You're not likely to attract others to God's blessings until you are blessed yourself. When people see God's joy and love and peace in you, they'll want to get it too, so don't let the enemy tell you you're selfish because you want God to bless you.

In *The Holy Spirit and You,* I use the illustration of a garden hose hanging on its rack. It's been raining a lot, and there's been no need to water the garden for a long time, so although there's been plenty of moisture outside, the poor hose is dry and dusty inside. It's attached to the water main, but the faucet isn't turned on. Now suppose there comes a dry season and you need to water the garden. You turn on the tap and what happens? The water first of all fills the hose. The hose can't water the garden until it's been filled with water itself. So the hose gets refreshed first, and then the water pours through the hose and out onto the garden. In a similar way, God wants to bless others through you, but first He wants to fill and bless you.

3

Speaking in Tongues

The Voice Is the Main Gate

Since the baptism with the Holy Spirit is an outflow, it's not surprising it should involve a special kind of speaking, because your voice is the main outlet of your whole being, through which you express yourself to God and to the world around you. The main way you share is by your voice. The miraculous ability to convey ideas to other people by talking, sets human beings apart from the rest of the living things on the earth. If an extra-terrestrial turned up, he might be a strange-looking creature, like E.T. in the movie, but if we found he could speak, we would treat him as a person, not an animal.

Words are powerful things. To put something into words is to make it real. To a great degree what you say makes you what you are. In the creation story it is God's words that bring things into being. God said, "Let there be light" and there was light. Psalm 8:2 says, "Out of the mouths of babes and sucklings hast thou ordained strength . . . that thou mightest still the enemy and the avenger." Proverbs 18:21 says, "Death and life are in the power of the tongue. . . ."

According to Jesus, if we *say* to a mountain, "Move!" it will move. We will have what we say. Even salvation itself is received by speaking. We must "confess with our lips" the Lord Jesus, which means we must *say* that we believe in Him. "With the mouth confession is made unto salvation" (Romans 10:10). (The Greek word translated "confession" means literally "to speak the same word.")

But we have abused the power to speak. The apostle James says, "The tongue is a flame of fire. It is full of wickedness, and poisons every part of the body. And the tongue is set on fire by hell itself, and can turn our whole lives into a blazing flame of destruction and disaster" (James 3:6, TLB). Remember, the apostle isn't speaking here to unbelievers, but to Christian brothers and sisters.

16

Don't you know how hard it is to control your tongue? Your speech needs to be tamed and purified before it can be used properly to speak to the Lord, or for the Lord. It isn't surprising, then, that the Holy Spirit would want to do something special about your voice.

The prophet Zephaniah foretells that God will "turn to the people a pure language, that they may all call upon the name of the Lord . . ." (Zephaniah 3:9).

And sure enough, when you read in the Scriptures about people receiving the power of the Holy Spirit, you find that they begin to speak in new languages. At least four times in the book of Acts it tells about people receiving the baptism in the Holy Spirit (Acts 2:4ff, 8:5-25; 10:44-48; 19:1-7). [Read these to the group if you have time.]

In three of these references it specifically says that as they received the baptism with the Holy Spirit they began to "speak in other languages, as the Spirit gave them to speak." The fourth example does not specifically mention speaking in new languages, but many leading commentators agree it was the speaking in tongues that attracted Simon Magus's attention and made him try to buy "the power" from Peter. For example, Matthew Henry, certainly an old and respected voice, says:

17

It is said, "The Holy Ghost was as yet fallen upon none of them," in those extraordinary powers which were conveyed by the descent of the Spirit upon the day of Pentecost. They were none of them endued with the gift of tongues, which seems then to have been the most usual immediate effect of the pouring out of the Spirit . . . This was both an eminent sign to those that believed not, and of excellent service to those that did . . . They laid their hands on them, to signify that their prayers were answered, and "that the gift of the Holy Ghost was conferred upon them" for upon the use of this sign, "they received the Holy Ghost, and spoke with tongues." *(Matthew Henry's Commentary,* Vol. VI, p. 100, Revell).

Other places in the Bible where speaking on tongues is mentioned, implied, or discussed are Isaiah 28:11-12 (cited by Paul in 1 Corinthians 14:21); Mark 16:17; Romans 8:26-27; 1 Corinthians 12:10, 13:1, 14:1-39; Jude 20. [If time permits, read some of these verses to the group.]

What is this speaking in new languages, or "speaking in tongues"? It simply means that if you have received Jesus, and therefore have the Holy Spirit living in you, He can give you words to speak in a language you do not understand, but which God understands.

The Two Ways of Speaking in Tongues

God uses this speaking in tongues in two different ways, and it's very important to see the difference. One is what we may call the "prayer language," and the other is the "gift of tongues."

One of the main reasons more Christians don't accept speaking in tongues is that they don't understand this difference. Even some popular translations of the Scriptures, such as the Jerusalem Bible, perpetuate the misunderstanding by calling all speaking in tongues "the gift of tongues." But the gift of tongues is a special kind of speaking in tongues in which someone brings words from God to a group of people. This message is specially given by the Spirit for the occasion, and requires an interpretation from the Holy Spirit so that it can be understood.

Paul has a lot to say about speaking in tongues in First Corinthians 12, 13, and 14, and all the way through these chapters he is moving back and forth between these two kinds of speaking in tongues. Unless you see the difference between them you will wonder how Paul can say in First Corinthians 12:30: "All don't speak in tongues, do they?" (AP), and then in First Corinthians 14:5 say, "I want you all to speak in tongues" (RSV), and in 14:23: "If the whole speaks with tongues," or in v. 29: "When you come together, every one of you has . . . a tongue." Or you won't know what Paul is talking about in verse 18, "1 thank God I speak in tongues more than any of you, but in an assembly I would rather speak five words with my intellect, than ten thousand in an unknown language" (AP)

We'll talk more about the *gift* of tongues a bit later, but right now we're going to talk about the *prayer language,* which is what you will be receiving tonight if you are baptized in the Spirit. This is a way of speaking in tongues which any believer can use at any time. The apostle Paul calls it "praying in the Spirit" (1 Corinthians 14:14-15) and this is what he is referring to when he says, "I want you all to speak in tongues" (1 Corinthians 14:5, RSV), or when he says, "I thank God I speak in tongues more than any of you" (14:18), or says that we should be "praying always with all prayer and supplication in the Spirit" (Ephesians 6:18).

The only reason all Christians don't use this ability is because they don't understand about it, and this is a great pity, because it's one of the most important and wonderful tools God has provided for us.

Praying in tongues, or "praying in the Spirit," again, simply means that you speak to God, but instead of using the words you know in your own language, you trust the Holy Spirit to give the words He chooses in whatever language He selects—perhaps in a brand new tongue that's never been spoken before.

It's a very simple thing. It's childlike. It does not involve a special ability or holiness. All you need is to have the Holy Spirit living in you, and be willing to trust Him to guide your voice as you speak. We often meet people who say they remember speaking in tongues when they were children, without knowing what it was. All they knew was it made them happy and close to God.

The wonderful thing is that when you begin to speak this way, you make a path for the Holy Spirit to move out from your innermost being (your spirit) to baptize (overwhelm) your soul (your psychological nature—intellect, will, and emotions) and your body (your physical nature). You are letting God have a greater influence over your whole being. "A person 'speaking in tongues' helps himself grow spiritually" (1 Corinthians 14:4, TLB). Remember we said that this is what *baptism* really means, allowing someone or something to overwhelm you—to come under their influence. So you can see why speaking in tongues is an integral part of the baptism with the Holy Spirit.

When you are baptized in the Spirit you will speak in tongues, and as you speak in tongues you will be baptized in the Holy Spirit, because you are allowing the Holy Spirit to gain a much deeper influence in your life as you surrender your speech to Him.

This is the way you allow God to tame your tongue, the "unruly member." You know we need to give everything to God, so why should it be surprising that we need to give Him our voices, too?

The apostle James compares the tongue to the bit in a horse's mouth. It's a small thing, he says, but it guides the whole horse. Or, he says, it's like the rudder of a big ship, which sets the course, even though it is small compared to the ship itself. James is here saying that if you could guide a person's tongue you could guide his whole being (see James 3:1-5).

This is the first and most important thing which happens when you speak in tongues. You don't have to speak in tongues to be saved, or to have the Holy Spirit living in you. You don't prove you have the Holy Spirit in you by speaking in tongues. If I want to know whether you have the Holy Spirit I don't ask you to speak in tongues, I ask, "Have you received Jesus as your Savior?" But speaking in tongues is the key to *releasing* the Holy Spirit, Who is already in you because you are a Christian.

Speaking in tongues isn't a sign or proof of holiness, but as you speak in tongues you will begin to be free in the Spirit.

EFFECTIVE COMMUNICATION

The new language the Spirit gives you helps you communicate with God more effectively, because it is God Himself Who is giving you the words. Again, Paul writes in Romans 8:26, "We are not able to make prayer to God in the right way; but the Spirit puts our desires into words which are not in our power to say" (New Testament in Basic English). Speaking in tongues makes you able to talk to God and praise Him exactly as He wants you to, which brings a more open relationship with Him.

Our language is limited. For example, look at the way we use the word *love*: "I love ice cream," "I love my dog," "I love my children," "I love my wife," "I love God." What different levels of meaning for that one word. There surely should be special words to tell God you love Him, and there are, but you don't know them, and cannot speak them with your intellect. God knows them, though, and can guide you to speak them in a language your mind doesn't understand. And when you speak them your spirit will be stirred because you are expressing yourself to God in a way you couldn't in your own tongue.

The same is true of inward sins and problems, which desperately need to be confessed to God so He can deal with them, but which you are not able to put into words. ". . . The Spirit puts our desires into words which are not in our power to say." (Romans 8:26, BE).

EFFECTIVE PRAYING

When you pray, you aren't tugging God's coattails to get Him to do what He really doesn't want to do! If God doesn't want it, you'd better not pray for it. Rather, when you pray you are going the way through your faith for God to work through your words, to get the things done He wants to do in a world that is still so much cut off from Him. You are functioning, so to speak, as God's executive. Remember, words are powerful, and God wants to use the power of the words you say to get His will done. Prayer is cooperating with God, so it helps a lot when you can pray exactly as He wants you to.

When you speak in tongues, you are praying exactly the way God needs you to pray, so you give Him a channel to work through that is much more open than when you try to express His will in your own language. For this reason, praying in tongues is a powerful means of intercession—praying for the

24

needs of other people and their circumstances. You will be surprised at the effectiveness of your prayers. And don't forget the other half of praying is listening. After you have prayed in the Spirit, you should stop and listen for what God may have to say to you.

WHY SHOULD I PRAY IN A LANGUAGE I DON'T UNDERSTAND?

And this is, of course, why God gives you a new language. When you speak in your prayer language, no one understands, including you (1 Corinthians 14:2). You can't modify or add to what you are saying when you're speaking in tongues, so your prayer comes right through the way God wants it.

This first kind of speaking in tongues, the prayer language, then, does three things:

1. It begins to set you free in the Spirit.

2. It helps you communicate with God in new freedom and so edifies or builds you up in your own spiritual life. It is a simple and refreshing way to pray, and it will bring rest to your soul.

3. It gives you the ability to pray more effectively to get God's will done in the world around you.

25

You Don't Have To Get Worked Up

Speaking in tongues has nothing to do with emotion. You may be relieved to know this, because maybe you thought you would have to get worked up in order to speak in tongues, and you were afraid you couldn't do it.

Your emotions are in your soul or *psyche,* and speaking in tongues doesn't come from your soul, but directly from the Holy Spirit, through your human spirit where the Holy Spirit is living. This is why Paul calls it "praying with the spirit" (1 Corinthians 14:14-15).

Some modern translations of the New Testament use the words "ecstasy" or "ecstatic," when referring to speaking in tongues, but these words are not in the Greek at all. They are not even implied.

The phrase "speaking in tongues" is simply an old-fashioned way of saying "speaking in languages." The word translated "tongue" in our English Bibles is the Greek word *glossa* which is the ordinary word for "language." If we want to be fancy, we still might say, "He speaks the English tongue." So "they began to speak in tongues" simply means "they began to speak in languages." You speak the language given by the Spirit just as you

26

would speak any other language. You don't have to get excited to do it.

Your emotions may or may not be touched by the Holy Spirit the first time you allow Him to give you the new language. You may feel nothing, you may feel a sense of refreshment and well-being, or you may feel absolutely overwhelmed by the joy of the Lord. It depends on things like your emotional makeup and training. If you have been taught to control your feelings and are afraid of letting go, for whatever reason, it may take awhile for the Holy Spirit to stir your emotions.

You don't *have* to feel anything in order for good things to begin to happen in your life, nor do you have to feel anything in order for your praying in the Spirit to be effective. You don't have to be feeling anything in order to be a good witness either. People will sense the Spirit in you, even though you yourself may be feeling "blah."

I'm not saying feelings are unimportant. They are very important. It would be terrible to have to live without emotions, but they are a result, not a cause. In other words, you don't experience God by getting emotional, but when you do experience Him, that certainly should stir your emotions. If you're not going to get excited about God, what are you going to get excited about?

27

THE GIFT OF TONGUES

After you have begun to use your prayer language, you will begin to see much more of the spiritual gifts that Paul lists in First Corinthians 12:4-11 at work in your life. These gifts are distributed by the Holy Spirit as *He* decides (12:11). Healings and miracles, knowledge and wisdom, discernment (the ability to detect right and wrong spiritual influences), prophecy (speaking words given by the Spirit in your own language), faith, tongues and interpretation, you may find any or all of these beginning to work through you. The potential to bring these gifts has been in you all the time since you accepted Jesus, and you may have experienced one or the other of them, but the release of the Spirit brings a far greater flow of the gifts. Most Christians are not aware of them at all until they have been baptized in the Spirit; in fact, a lot of good earnest believers have given up on them entirely, and will tell you they are "not for today," but were just for Bible times. But many millions of Christians can testify that Jesus is still doing His mighty works in the world today, through the faith and prayers of His people.

One of these spiritual gifts is the gift of tongues. We said earlier that this is the second way of speaking in tongues. Like the other gifts, it is given only when and as the Holy Spirit decides, and through whomever He decides. This gift of tongues

28

is given when God has something He wants to say to His people when they are meeting together. Paul is referring to this kind of speaking in tongues in First Corinthians 12 when he asks "all don't speak in tongues, do they?"; and again in First Corinthians 14:27 when he says that only two or three people should speak in tongues in the course of a meeting, and then only if they are interpreted, so that everyone can understand what God is saying to the people in the group.

With the prayer language you can speak in tongues any time you decide to do so, but you do not just decide you'd like to bring a gift of tongues. The Holy Spirit has to let you know He wants you to. If you started to speak out in tongues in a meeting without being specially moved by the Spirit to do so, you would just be praying out loud in your prayer language. A group of people praying individual prayers together out loud in tongues can be edifying, provided everyone present understands what is happening. They would not be bringing *gifts* of tongues, however. This is what Paul is writing about in 1 Corinthians 14:16, 23 and 28. But if the Spirit moves someone to bring a gift of tongues, He will provide the interpretation, either through that same person, or another.

This kind of speaking in tongues can be very beautiful and inspiring; and it can be just the opposite if it isn't used properly. People will sometimes use the gift of tongues as an opportunity

29

to be very demonstrative (Paul warns the Corinthians about this very thing in First Corinthians 14:22, 26, 33, 40) and this is why many church leaders are afraid of speaking in tongues. Not understanding the difference between the prayer language and the gift of tongues, they think that if people start praying in tongues, they will speak out noisily in church, and create disorder.

Now, of course, public gifts of tongues should not be disorderly or distressing. You may or may not ever be inspired by the Holy Spirit to bring a gift of tongues in a meeting, but if you are, be sure first of all that you are at the right time and place. Remember you are in control of the way the spiritual gifts are used. "The spirits of the prophets are subject to the prophets" (1 Corinthians 14:32).

Many think speaking in tongues refers to an outburst that just sort of "happens" to people, and that it may "happen" to them. They think they will suddenly be taken over by the Holy Spirit against their will, and perhaps to their embarrassment. All this is simply not so. You will not suddenly be compelled to speak out in church. You won't start speaking loudly in tongues in the supermarket. The Holy Spirit does not coerce or compel. Again, Paul says the "spirit of the prophet is subject to the prophet." He also says, "I will pray with my spirit," that is, "I do it at my will—when I decide to." (1 Corinthians 14:15, 32).

No matter how inspired you may be, you would be out of order to bring a gift of tongues in your church on Sunday morning if the congregation would not understand, or would be frightened or turned off by it, or if it would be against the wishes of the pastor, or would embarrass or anger him. After church one Sunday morning, one of my friends said to me, "I really felt inspired to speak in tongues during the service, but I thought people would not understand, so I whispered the message to the person I knew who was sitting next to me, and he whispered the interpretation back to me."

There are other varieties of the gift of tongues, such as when a person speaks in a human language (like French or German) he or she does not know, but which someone else present understands because they speak it. Some of the people on the Day of Pentecost were doing this. "How is it that we hear them speaking in our languages the wonderful works of God?" (Acts 2:11). This happens fairly often these days, too.

I have myself spoken in tongues in Japanese and in Nepali. I don't know either language, but in both cases others present recognized them, and translated them. I have heard a man speak beautifully in Spanish and then French, neither of which tongue he knew. I know very little Spanish, although I recognized a few words, but the French was said very clearly and slowly:

"C'est bon, cest bon. Tres bon et le bon Dieu," which means "It's good. It's good. Very good is the good God.

A member of my parish, well known to me, on several occasions spoke perfectly in Mandarin, and was understood by Chinese people who heard him. I have known others to speak Latin, Hebrew, Korean, old French, Basque, when they did not know those languages, but people present did. [You may know examples in your own experience, or you may use mine if you wish.]

Please remember again, we are not talking about *getting* the Holy Spirit, but *releasing* Him to function as He wants to, releasing Him to fill other rooms in your house of life. If you don't speak in your prayer language right away, it isn't because God isn't giving you that gift, but because for some reason you are inhibited. Keep working on it. Something is getting in the way. Find out. Don't give up on it. *Speaking in tongues is vitally important to your Christian life.*

[Emphasize strongly to the people that speaking in tongues is an integral part of receiving the baptism with the Holy Spirit. You will need to be definite about it, as many are saying you don't really need to speak in tongues.]

4

PREPARING TO RECEIVE THE BAPTISM WITH THE HOLY SPIRIT

The first and all-essential prerequisite to receiving the baptism is to receive Jesus as your Savior.

[Never, never, pray for yourself or anyone else to be baptized in the Spirit unless you are sure, as much you reasonably can be, that you, he, or she has accepted Jesus, because that is when the Holy Spirit comes to live in us.]

If you do not make sure of this, you may find yourself praying with someone who is not a Christian, and not only does not have the Holy Spirit living in him, but is indwelt by a spirit other than the Spirit of

God. When you encourage such a person to "release the spirit" this other thing may manifest itself, perhaps in a weird or even frightening way. You may find yourself having to take authority over it, perhaps upsetting other people who are praying, to say nothing of the fear it may cause the person you are praying with. In the earlier years of renewal, and still in many places, people were and are prayed for not only without any preparation, but without even being asked if they know Jesus.

[So stop at this point and give them a chance to be sure they have received Jesus and the forgiveness of their sins, and have been reborn of the Holy Spirit. There are people who have belonged to church all their lives, but have never received Jesus personally. Don't assume just because a person is a faithful church member or even a clergyman, that he or she has accepted Jesus. And certainly don't assume someone has accepted the Lord just because he or she is attending a Christian meeting or conference.]

Prayer to Receive Jesus

Say something like: Would you please close your eyes, and keep them closed for a little while. This is so that no one will be embarrassed or inhibited. [Keep your own eyes open so that you can direct what is to take place. Then continue something like this]:

While you have your eyes closed, I want to ask whether you remember specifically a time when you received Jesus as your Lord and Savior and asked him to come into your life. I'm not asking whether you believe in God. You wouldn't be here unless you did. I'm not asking whether you belong to a church, or are active in Christian work, I'm asking whether you have accepted Jesus, person to person. Some folks still have their religion in the name of their parents, or their church or their pastor. Have you established your own relationship with the Lord?

I'm not asking whether you *felt* anything happened, or *feel* He is living in you, but just whether you have ever asked Him to, because if you did, He came, whether you have been aware of Him or not.

Any of you here who are not sure you have personally said "yes" to Jesus, and would like to do so now, please raise your right hand as though you were voting "yes." I'm not going to ask you to come forward, or embarrass you in some way. At this point it's between you and Jesus. Please don't hesitate to do this.

[Pause here to give people an opportunity to raise their hands. It is good to acknowledge each hand as it is raised, so people will know they have the Lord."]

Now those of you who have raised your hands, please follow me in this prayer. Make it your own prayer. Others of you may join in if you wish. There's nothing wrong with reaffirming your commitment to the Lord:

Dear God, I believe Jesus is Your only begotten Son, Who came to us as a human being. I believe He died on the Cross, and poured out His life's blood to take away the sin of the world. I believe that He rose from death to give us resurrection life.

Lord God, I confess to You all the wrong things I've done, all the sin and guilt and fear in my life. Please forgive me and wash me in Jesus' precious blood. I believe You are doing this right now. 1, accept Your forgiveness. Thank You, Father. Thank You Jesus? [Pause.]

Dear Jesus, I open my life to You. Come in, Lord Jesus. I receive You as my Savior and King. Come and live in me, and give me Your Holy Spirit. Thank You, Lord. I believe You are living in me now, and I am born again of the Spirit. I have a new kind of life in me, resurrection life. Thank You, Father. Thank You, Jesus. Thank You, Holy Spirit. Praise the Lord.

If you've never asked Him before to come into your life, you can be certain that you have asked Him

36

now, and that He has come. Because of Jesus, the Holy Spirit is living in you and you can release His power in your life. You might want to make a permanent record of the date somewhere, so you can remember exactly when you received Jesus as your Lord and Savior.

CHECK YOUR ATTITUDES

You are going to invite the Holy Spirit, Who is living in your spirit, to flow out and fill or baptize your soul and body, so this is a good time to look and see whether there is anything that might get in His way. After all, going back to the illustration of the friend visiting at your house, it would be nice to rid of anything in your house that might offend him.

Do you have an attitude in your life which you know the Holy Spirit cannot accept, and which you need to correct? The most common one is unforgiveness. Is there someone you have not forgiven? Do you say of somebody who has wronged you, "Oh, I don't hate him, I just don't want to have anything to do with him."

Don't play games with the Lord. Jesus says very clearly that if we don't forgive others, God can't forgive us. "Whenever you stand praying, forgive, if you have anything against anyone; so that your Father also who is in heaven may forgive you your trespasses" (Mark 11:25, RSV).

"Oh," you may say, "if you only knew what happened. I just can't forgive him after what he did to me."

Well, then, say to God, "Lord, I honestly don't feel I can forgive him—and I really don't want to, but since I know You want me to, all I can say is I *want* to want to."

God will accept this, and before you realize it, you will find yourself forgiving and releasing that person. You can even say, "I wish I wanted to want to forgive him," and God will take you up on it, and help you to forgive all the way. God likes us to be honest with Him. If you find you just can't bring yourself to forgive at all, you need more healing in your soul. Find some good books on the subject and read about it, and find someone to pray with you about it. Unforgiveness will block your release in the Holy Spirit.

There are other wrong attitudes: bad temper, discouragement, negativity, resentment, worry, sexual problems, and so forth. You can't just wave your hands and get rid of these things, but you can stop excusing them, and release them to the Lord. If you have a bad temper you can stop excusing it, and instead ask God to heal your bad temper, and forgive you for the times you have lost it.

If you have a problem with your sexual orientation, you need to stop claiming that God made you that way, and recognize instead that you need healing (and forgiveness, if you have put your inclinations into action).

38

Don't excuse problems as "alternative life styles."
God only accepts one life style, the life style of Jesus.
As you admit to God that you have problems, He will
show you how to deal with them. He knows that you
cannot get rid of them by yourself, but He cannot help
you with them if you hang on to them and excuse them.
So release them to the Lord as you remember them,
and let Him deal with them. Offer them to Him, and
the way will be cleared for the Holy Spirit to be able to
move freely in your soul.

What about the things you can't remember? As
you go along in your walk in the Spirit, watch for the
Lord to show you hidden areas of your personality that
He wants to heal. The more you get healed, the more
you will get free in the Spirit. All of us have deep hurts
that we are not conscious of, but which can and do
interfere with the flow of the Spirit in us. Jesus wants
to heal them, but can only do so as we allow Him to.
We have them locked up and need to open them to Him.
Some people's souls are so hurt they have to be healed
before they can release the Holy Spirit at all. Again,
this is where soul-healing prayer can really help.

Let's stop and pray right now about these things.
Will you please close your eyes so no one will feel
self-conscious? Now, if you remember or recognize
some wrong attitude in your life that needs to be
corrected, will you raise your hand?

Let's all pray together. You follow me as I pray, but make it your own prayer:

Dear Father, I recognize that I do have wrong attitudes in my life, and especially I remember the following ones.

At this point just tell God what the things are you want to release to Him.

[Pause here for a few moments.]

I do release these things to You, Father, and I ask You to forgive me for them, and for any other sin in my life. I receive Your forgiveness, and ask You to make me more like Jesus. And any spirits associated with any of these things, in Jesus' Name I bind you. I cast you away from my life, never to return. In Jesus' Name and under His precious blood. Amen.

If you remember someone you have not forgiven, name that person, and ask God to help you forgive him or her, or to help you *want* to forgive them. [You may want to have the people pray together, pausing for them to name—quietly to themselves—the person or persons they want to forgive.]

Dear Father, you know I have been holding anger against [have them insert name of person or persons] *and I now release them to you, and forgive them. I ask you to bless them, heal them, and bring them to know*

40

you through Jesus Christ, if they don't already. I release them, and I release myself from all hatred or unforgiveness. In Jesus' Name. [You may want to have the people pray this prayer all together, pausing for them to name the person or persons they want to forgive.]

5

Two Other Areas

There are two other areas we need to talk about before we pray for the release of the Holy Spirit. They may not apply to you directly, but you need to know about them, and what to do about them. You should never pray for yourself, or anyone else, to receive the baptism with the Holy Spirit unless these things have been dealt with.

The first one is, have you been involved in any other religion besides Christianity or Judaism? In the United States usually this means one of the made-up modern religions or philosophies that we usually call *cults*. Of course, many of the cults draw their inspiration from the old paganisms. Transcendental Meditation, for example, is a modern cult, but it is really a form of Mantra Yoga Hinduism.

Most cults teach that Jesus is a great leader, teacher, or prophet, but not that He is really and truly divine. They usually do not believe that He rose physically from the dead, although some believe in a spiritual resurrection. They will not usually believe that He died so that our sins could be forgiven.

Most cults claim that sin, if it exists, must be dealt with by our own efforts, either in this life or by being reborn on this earth in some other body (reincarnation). Others say that sin and sickness are just an error of your mortal mind, and that if you get your thinking straightened out all will be well.

The cults often claim to be forms of Christianity, but their teachings are very different from those of the Bible. For example, one of the most subtle of the cults, and also one of the most powerful, which is thought of by many as a Christian denomination, says that Jesus is a divine Person, and "an important Member of the Trinity," but you soon discover that they also believe that Jesus became who He is by keeping the "precepts of the Gospel"— by which they mean the teachings of their cult. According to them, salvation comes through keeping these precepts, not through receiving Jesus as Savior.

Jesus is, they say, an example that men can become "almighty gods" by keeping the teachings of their cult. According to them, these "god-men" will be given their own planets to rule. Some of them believe that Adam became the "almighty god" of planet earth. A man can have many wives, they say. (They believe that Jesus was married to three women), and they believe that a man, having become a god, can then resurrect the wives he liked, and populate his own planet with the children he begets by his wives, to all eternity.

Well-known cults include Christian Science, Latter Day Saints (Mormons), Jehovah's Witnesses, Subud, Bahai, Soka Gakkai, Yoga, Scientology, Transcendental Meditation, Swedenborgianism, etc. You will find a more complete list at the end of the book, which you are free to copy and distribute if you wish.

Don't confuse cults with sects. A sect is a *section* of a particular religion. Every Christian denomination, Protestant and Catholic, is a sect of Christianity. But there are Christian sects that emphasize some special teaching so as to exclude those who don't agree with them and join them, believing that only those who accept their teachings are going to be saved, or are going to have special privileges in the Kingdom.

These exclusive sects are not cults in the usual sense of the word, but they may exaggerate some teaching to the point that it becomes cultic in effect.

45

Some sects, for example, while believing in Jesus as Savior, deny the Trinity of God, saying that Jesus is Himself the Father, Son, and Holy Spirit. Other insist that only those who have received water baptism according to a precise ceremony and form of words are truly saved. Others may say that everyone must be subject to a particular line of authority, or that only those who observe Saturday as the Sabbath will be in the first resurrection.

The problem with these exclusive sects is not so much that they hold these teachings themselves, but that they insist everyone else must join them and believe as they do. If you belong or have belonged to one of these, you need to renounce anything in the teachings that is contrary to the plain truths of the Scriptures.

Besides the modern cults, there are the old religions, Buddhism, Hinduism, Islam, Taoism, etc. This includes the religions of such cultures as the Hawaiian, the American Indian, the Eskimo, and others. People should value their heritage, but if the religion of a particular nationality or race is against the will and word of the true God, it must be renounced. This is not racism. The truth of Jesus has nothing to do with race or nationality. Unfortunately, Christianity is often thought of as the religion of the Caucasians, which is rather strange, because Jesus was not a European, but a man of the

Middle East, and in today's world Christianity seems to be growing most rapidly among non-Caucasians.

Usually pagan religions involve worship of demonic spirits, and this can't be mixed with Christianity, although it's often been tried. Overseas you encounter these other religions quite often. In the United States it isn't too likely that you or the people you are talking to will have been brought up in one of the old religions, although it might be so among the American Indians, Eskimo, or Hawaiians, or in, an ethnic church group.

There are an increasing number of people in the United States, especially in the entertainment field and certain racial groups, who are turning to these old religions and adopting Islam, Hinduism or Buddhism, or one of the ethnic beliefs. In some places the old festivals and idols are being revived, involving worship of the ancient gods and goddesses. These historic non-Christian religions must be renounced, just as the cults must be renounced, if people have become involved with them.

Judaism is a special case. It is not a pagan religion, of course. It is the root from which the flower of Christianity has grown. A Jew does not need to renounce Judaism, but does need to be sure he has accepted the Lord Jesus as Messiah, and thus has become a "completed Jew," and knows and accepts that he cannot be saved by the old law, but through faith in Jesus.

People sometimes commit themselves to philosophical or psychological systems such as those of Carl Jung, or Teilhard de Chardin, as if they were religions. The teachings of such men may contain true concepts, but we are to be disciples of Jesus, not of any human being, and our basic source book is the Scriptures. If a person has made a commitment to one of these human systems, it should be renounced, too.

If at any time in your life you have been in one of the cults, or the pagan religions, you must renounce this involvement before you ask for the release of the Holy Spirit. This is true even if you've long since given up believing in that cult or religion. You need specifically to cast all its influence away from you. If you don't, when you release the Holy Spirit to fill your soul and body, you may have a distressing internal battle that can cause depression and confusion and erratic behavior, in extreme cases even going so far as actual breakdown. This may not only trouble you, but upset and frighten people who are watching you. The Holy Spirit eventually will win, and the confusion will clear up, but why go through it? Take care of the problem before you pray.

The Occult

The other area to be dealt with is the occult. This includes such things as mind-reading (telepathy), extrasensory perception (ESP), clairvoyance ("second sight"), mind-over-matter (psychokinesis or telekinesis), astrology (horoscopes), fortune-telling (precognition) and all the various practices associated with it-reading tea-leaves, palm-reading, crystal balls, Ouija boards, Tarot cards and other fortunetelling by cards, I Ching, and so forth. It includes any attempt to contact spirits other than God-any kind of spiritualism or spiritism—or dealings with so-called psychic phenomena.

The word *occult* means *hidden*. When the human race turned away from God, Satan took control and set up his own dark spiritual realm, which we call the *psychic world*. He filled it with what the Apostle Paul calls "powers and authorities," "world-rulers of this darkness," "wicked spirits in the heavenlies" (Ephesians. 6:12, LG). If you try to use occult power you will make contact with this dark world. You will open the way for wrong spirits to oppress and trouble your soul. The darkness can get into your mind and emotions, giving you ideas and feelings that interfere with or oppose the work of the Holy Spirit. If you have taken part in the occult at any time in your life from childhood on, you must renounce it.

It is not possible to explain everything about the cults and the occult at this time. If you have difficulty with what I am saying, or are offended by it, please do *not* pray to receive the baptism with the Holy Spirit until you have investigated further and are clearly ready to renounce the cults and the occult. It is psychologically and spiritually dangerous to mix the teachings of the cult with the power of the Holy Spirit, as some of these other beliefs have powerful demonic forces associated with them. It is dangerous to try to do business with the devil's psychic realm and at the same time try to receive the power of God's Holy Spirit. It is inviting the forces of light and darkness to use your soul for a battleground. If you cannot remember any specific involvement with these things, pray the prayer anyway, and offer to God anything that might be there even though you cannot remember it.

Also, if you know that your parents, grandparents, or great-grandparents were involved in the occult, renounce any influence that might have come down to you from them. Place the Cross of Jesus and the blood of Jesus between you and any wrong influence from former generations.

As time goes by, you may recall things you had forgotten that need to be dealt with. If you do, simply renounce them then and there, using the same prayers we are using tonight. [You will find a list of the cults, pagan religions, and common occult practices in the appendices. If an overhead projector is available you could display them. Failing that, you could make copies of the list to distribute.]

How to Pray to Renounce False Teachings

Again close your eyes so no one will feel exposed. Now, if you remember you have been involved in the cults or the occult, and need to renounce them, please raise your hand. I'm not going to embarrass you, so don't hesitate to take part. [Usually a lot of people raise their hands at this point.]

Everybody join in this prayer, whether you can specifically remember anything or not:

Dear Father, if I have believed, or accepted, or taught, or taken part in teachings or practices contrary to Your will or Your Word, or in any other way displeasing to You, I am truly sorry, and I ask You to forgive me in the Name of Jesus. I especially remember these: _____.

51

Now, quietly, between you and the Lord, tell Him what it is you need to renounce or get rid of from your life. If you remember having taken part in one of the cults or the occult at any time in your life, quietly tell God what it is.

[Pause here to give people a chance to pray to themselves, privately, and then have them continue with this prayer:]

I do renounce these things, Lord, in the Name of Jesus and under His precious blood. With Your help, I promise You I will not engage in them any more. I bind them and cast them out of my life, never to return, in Jesus' Name.

And any spirits associated with any of these things, in Jesus' Name I bind you. I cast you out of my life, never to return, in Jesus' Name and under His precious blood. Amen!

[Now you, the leader, say this prayer for everyone:]

Dear Father, if anything has been cast out of us by means of these prayers, please fill the empty space with your Holy Spirit. In Jesus' Name. Amen.

6

A Pause for Redeployment

[This brief chapter is addressed to you, the leader.]

At this point take time for people to rearrange
themselves so you can easily reach those who want to
receive the baptism in the Holy Spirit, to help and
encourage them. Ask the people who want to pray to
raise their hands. If the group is small or the seating
can be moved around, have those who want to receive
come and sit in the front, bringing their chairs with
them if need be.

If you are in a church or auditorium with fixed
seats, estimate how many rows it will take to
accommodate the people who raised their hands,

allowing for an empty row of seats between each occupied row to let helpers reach people without stumbling over feet. Then ask the people sitting in the front rows who are not asking to be prayed with to please move further back in the auditorium so as to leave enough front rows clear for the people who do. (Whew! Are you still with me?) In other words, arrange it so that those asking for the baptism in the Spirit are seated in the first, third and fifth rows, and so forth; the second, fourth, etc., should be left vacant.

Should you ask people to kneel? If there are kneelers, as in some churches, folks may of course kneel if they wish to. If it is the custom in the particular church to have people come and kneel at the altar rail, that's fine too. I do not recommend that people kneel with their heads in the seats of their chairs or pews, and their backs to the front of the church, as many are used to doing. This position is okay for personal prayer, but makes it extremely awkward to talk or pray with people.

Even though in my own denomination we usually kneel to pray in church, I actually believe that sitting is the best posture for receiving the Spirit, and of course I have scriptural precedent, for Acts 2:2 says that at Pentecost the Holy Spirit "filled all the house where they were sitting." Sitting is relaxed, and you want people to feel relaxed. In the last analysis, of course, let people be in the attitude in which they feel most at ease.

When everyone is reshuffled, you might want to sing a song or two to bring things back together, and then continue.

7

How to Receive the Release of the Holy Spirit

Remember that you are going to receive the baptism with the Holy Spirit. Receiving is something you do. I can offer you a five-dollar bill, but unless you receive it, I cannot do anything more about it. I cannot *receive* you the five dollars, I can only give it to you. You must receive it. So it is with the Holy Spirit. God *gave* you the Holy Spirit when you *received* Jesus. He cannot give Him to you again. Now you must receive the Gift that you already have been given.

[As a visual aid you may want actually to offer to give someone a five-dollar bill, while you are making this point, showing that although you are offering it to them, unless they reach out and take it, they haven't received it. You can only *give* it to them, you can't *receive* it for them.]

How Do You Receive the Baptism in the Spirit?

How do you *receive?* Just as they did in the New Testament: "They began to speak in other languages as the Spirit gave them utterance" (Acts 2:4). 1 don't know any other way to tell you to go about it. Speaking in tongues is the golden key that unlocks your spirit to allow the Holy Spirit to flow out and baptize the rest of your being.

Some will say, "I want to receive the Holy Spirit by faith. " That's fine, if you know that faith is something you do. It means actively trusting God. If Peter had stayed in the boat saying, "I have faith that I can walk on water." but didn't do anything, one of the other disciples would certainly have said, "If you've got faith, Peter, get out of the boat and let's see your faith by your action." "Faith without works is dead" (James 2:20). "Faith without action is dead."

To speak in tongues you have to "get out of the boat," that is, take a step of faith, and begin to speak, just as Peter began to walk. Peter had known how to walk ever since he was a small child, and you have known how to speak ever since you were very little. Peter walked, doing what he knew how to do, while trusting Jesus to hold him up on the water. You are going to speak, doing what you know how to do, while trusting Jesus to give you the words. Speaking in tongues is just as definitely something you do, as speaking any other language. God does not speak in tongues, and He isn't going to *make you* speak, as if He were a ventriloquist, and you a dummy.

God won't treat you that way; He respects your free will. Besides, it would not be an act of faith if you had to wait for God to make you speak. Peter did not wait for Jesus to come and pick him up and walk him on the water, but began to do what he, Peter, knew he could do, and that was to walk. Jesus had said, "Come," so Peter came. He walked, trusting Jesus, and so walked on the water. If Peter had not stepped out of the boat in faith and started walking, he would never have walked on the water.

In the same way, until you open your mouth and begin to speak, you will not speak in tongues. Some people think they need to *fall under the power* to speak in tongues. Falling under the power, which means someone being so overcome by the power and glory of God that he drops to the floor, may happen sometimes when a person feels the power of the Spirit. It may happen when praying for healing, and it may happen when someone is praying to be baptized in the Spirit, but you don't *have* to fall under the power to speak in tongues, any more than

59

you have to fall under the power to be healed. Going down under the power is a response to the overwhelming love of God, and it can certainly make a person receptive to blessings from the Spirit, but it isn't a necessity. The Scriptures do not mention people falling down under the power when they were baptized in the Spirit. Some of them may have done so, of course, but it is not recorded and so cannot be taken as a pattern to follow.

Then, too, people who fall under the power while praying to be released in the Holy Spirit will sometimes mistake that experience itself for the baptism in the Spirit, and will not go on to speak in tongues. So if someone does fall during prayer for the release of the Spirit, be sure you encourage him to begin to use his prayer language.

You start speaking in tongues the same way you start speaking any language, by beginning to make sounds. You would never speak at all if you were not willing to make sounds. A baby learning to talk doesn't have any words in his memory, so he just begins to make noises that later will become meaningful. When you speak a language you know, you have the words stored in your memory, and use them to guide your voice. When you speak in tongues, though, like the baby, you are just making sounds; you don't have the words of the new language in your memory with which to guide your tongue.

The Holy Spirit is ready to provide the words, however, so the sounds you speak will take the form He wants them to take, and mean what He wants them to mean. You are really being childlike when you speak in tongues, and this, of course, is exactly what Jesus said we should do—become "as little children" (Matthew 18:3). So another thing speaking in tongues does for us is humble our intellectual pride. Modern man wants to understand and control everything with his mind, but when you speak in tongues you act with childlike simplicity, trusting God and not your own cleverness.

On the other hand, even though you are using the words the Spirit is giving you, you are the one doing the speaking. It's something like a pianist choosing to play the music of, say, Johann Sebastian Bach. The music being played is a Bach fugue. The pianist is following the music of Bach, but he or she is still in complete control, and is free to play the piece fast or slow, loudly or softly, an octave higher or an octave lower. The only limitation is that as long as he or she has decided to play the Bach fugue, the pianist is receiving the music the composer gave when he wrote the piece. He may decide not to play that selection, and may decide to improvise one of his own, but if he wishes to play Bach, he will have to follow Bach's music. Yet in no way is he compelled to do so.

In somewhat the same way, when you decide to speak in tongues, you can start and stop whenever you want. You can speak loudly or softly, high or low, quickly or slowly, but if you wish to speak in the language the Lord provides, you will have to follow His score, His script, and speak the words He offers. The difference is that God does not usually spread the score out in front of you, but asks you to trust Him for each syllable as it comes, as you speak. (There are exceptions. Sometimes a person will hear the words coming to his mind ahead of time. If this happens to you, go ahead and speak them out. Occasionally someone will see the words written as on a blackboard or what looks like a ticker tape. If this happens, read them off.)

Perhaps you once dreamed you were speaking in tongues. This is wonderful, but now you need to trust God and speak in tongues while you are awake.

When you begin to speak in any language, you start by making a sound, and that sound becomes the first syllable of what you are going to say. It's the same with beginning to speak in tongues. You begin by uttering a sound—whatever sound comes to your lips first. One syllable spoken in faith can begin to set your spirit free, and change your life. But you have to begin to speak. When you speak that first sound, trusting God to make sense of it, it becomes the first syllable of your tongue. You have *begun* to speak in the language God has for you. Go on with the next syllable, and the next as they come, and the language will begin to flow.

This is not a test of your spirituality. It isn't an exam you can flunk. The only thing being tested here is your level of inhibition. Speaking in the Spirit doesn't show how holy you are and you don't do it to prove you have the Holy Spirit living in you. Remember, if I want to find out whether you have the Holy Spirit living in you, I won't ask you to speak in tongues, I will ask you, "Have you received Jesus as your Savior?"

Speaking in tongues, or praying in the Spirit, as Paul calls it, is something you are able to do *because* you have the Holy Spirit in you. Every Christian has the ability to speak in tongues and receive the baptism in the Holy Spirit. You just need to be childlike and trust God. Allow the Holy Spirit to guide your voice, your chief means of expression. It's just as if you were making a good friend really welcome as a guest at your house; you would give him full permission to use the telephone or drive your car.

Satan has two comments he will try on you at this point if he can. The first is "That's not it," and if you are listening to yourself critically, and watching how you feel or sound, this may be an easy point for him to make. Pay no attention to him. Just keep on with what you are doing. If what you're doing isn't "it," what are you going to do about it?

But what you're saying is "it," because speaking in tongues begins when you begin to make sounds, trusting God. The first syllable you utter in faith is the beginning of speaking in the Spirit. It doesn't matter a bit what it is, or what it sounds like. It's the beginning of your prayer language.

The other comment Satan often makes is, "That's just you speaking." The answer is obvious, "Who did you think it was going to be?" Remember, God doesn't speak in tongues. He is guiding you to speak, so of course it is "just you" speaking. You are doing the speaking, and God is doing the guiding and inspiring. If you were praying in English and someone came by and said, "That's just you praying, you know," you'd say, "Of course it is." and pay no further attention. That's what you need to do here, too.

When you begin to speak, keep on going. Speak for ten or fifteen minutes, and more if there's time. When you go home after the meeting, keep on speaking. And each day keep on praying in the Spirit as much and as often as you can.

On the Day of Pentecost, they received by "beginning to speak" and that's exactly what I invite you to do right now. We're going to ask Jesus to baptize you, and you then need to *receive* that baptism by opening your mouth and taking the step of faith we talked about. God will honor your trusting Him.

It doesn't matter what sounds you make first, just as it didn't matter whether Peter put his left or right foot onto the water first, but you *must begin to make sounds.* This is your step out of the boat. Remember, you are going to do the talking, not God. Whatever sounds you make, accept them, and go on speaking.

Pay no attention to how you feel. You are talking to your Father in heaven and telling Him things He knows you need to say to Him. You may or may not feet any inspiration or uplift, or anything at all, or you may get a free trip to the third heaven. You may be moved to laugh or cry for joy. Do it. Express your feelings, while remembering to be thoughtful of other people around you. Don't frighten them with your enthusiasm, but do enjoy yourself.

You may, like me, feel nothing when you first begin to speak in the Spirit. That's all right. Remember, your emotions are in your soul, and sometimes it takes a while for the Spirit to reach them. Don't worry about it.

[You've done the instructing; now people need to be encouraged to follow through, pray in tongues, and receive the baptism in the Holy Spirit. If someone says, "I am baptized in the Holy Spirit already, I just haven't spoken in tongues," don't stop to argue with them at this point, just urge them to speak in tongues. The Lord will show them why it's important. If a person asks for further explanations at this point, have someone go and talk with them away from the main group so as not to distract the others.]

8

TRAINING PEOPLE TO HELP YOU

[A chapter addressed to you.]

It's really important to have people helping you when you come to the prayer time, especially if the group is large. You need to be wise about this, though, or it may do more harm than good. It's good, if you can, to have a training session ahead of time to prepare helpers. In any case, don't let anyone help you pray unless they have been listening to your teaching to the group, or are familiar with your approach. Naturally you shouldn't have someone praying who has not yet received the baptism in the Spirit. Be sure that you and those assisting are free in your own prayer languages, as it really helps the others if you speak in tongues yourself as you encourage them to do so.

Beware of letting just anyone come and help. If you do, you will get some who will use the time-honored methods that don't work very well. You will get those who feel people should get worked up and make a lot of noise. You may get the ones who say "imitate my tongue," or who suggest to the person words to say, and you'll probably get some jaw jigglers and head massagers. Also you will get the friends of poor old John who has been seeking the baptism in the Spirit for twenty years, and they've been *helping* him, and the big thing he needs is to get away from the well meant ministrations of those same friends.

The Main Points

These are the main things you want your helpers to know about, and they also apply to you, of course, as you pray with the people:

Stand in front of the person you are praying with, where you can be seen and heard, and where you can talk to them easily and naturally. Don't stand behind—this is not nearly as effective. You may lay your hand gently on his or her head or shoulder. Pray aloud in your own prayer language. Not only does this allow the Spirit to give you the right prayer for the person, it also gives him or her a background of prayer to join in with. As he or she begins to speak in tongues, no matter what little sounds may be coming, or even if you can only see the lips moving, say, "Wonderful. That's great. Praise the Lord. Keep it up."

Do not give people something to say, or invite them to imitate you. True, it will often work, because it does get things started, but it can make trouble later, as the enemy will tell them they were not really speaking in tongues, but just copying you. Also since those who oppose speaking in tongues often maintain people are simply imitating others, don't strengthen that false impression.

The most common reason people don't begin to speak in tongues is that they hesitate to begin to make sounds. Try to persuade them to begin, even if it is an "oh" or an "ah" or just a sigh, or even a groan. Point out that the Scriptures tell us "Open thy mouth wide, and I will fill it" (Psalm 81:10b), and to "Make a joyful noise unto the Lord" (Psalm 100: 1, and others). If people once get the idea they need to begin to make sounds, they will usually start to speak in tongues. Don't try to get them excited or noisy, but do tell them to speak loudly enough to hear themselves. Point out to them that they must stop speaking English, or any other language they know, before they can begin to speak in tongues. You can't talk two languages at once. You can't pray with the Spirit and with the intellect at the same time—although you can do it alternately (1 Corinthians 14:15).

If you encounter someone who after a reasonable time does not seem to be willing or able to open his mouth and begin to speak, do not hassle him. Do not give him what a friend calls a "Pentecostal massage". Just say, "You may be feeling inhibited and shy. That's okay." Encourage person to go home and keep trying to speak in the Spirit. People often begin to speak when they are occupied in doing something else—taking a shower, vacuuming the rug, driving the car. Remind him again that he already has the Holy Spirit in him. He's just having difficulty allowing Him to guide his speech.

Once in awhile you will find someone who just will not do what you say, who will insist on speaking English (or some other language known to him), or who will not open his mouth at all, because he insists. God must do the talking. The person will sometimes say, "I don't want this to be in the flesh, I want it to be from the Lord." Say to him, "If you are doing something 'in the flesh,' that means you're not trusting God, but trying to do it yourself. When you step out in faith and trust God to guide you as you speak in tongues, that's the very opposite of being 'in the flesh.' The flesh does not want to act in faith. It wants things proven to it. To wait for God to *make* you speak is operating 'in the flesh.'"

These people may be having trouble because they do not yet understand what the Scriptures are saying. If it's obvious you are at a standstill with them, suggest they go home and read *The Holy Spirit and You* (published by Bridge-Logos Publishers) carefully, especially the chapters on preparing to receive and receiving the baptism with the Holy Spirit.

Sometimes someone will have difficulty speaking because he or she (in this case we'll say it's a woman, although it might just as well be a man) has gone through a time of extreme tension, and is afraid to let go. A recent serious illness, or the illness or death of someone close, a divorce, unemployment, or other stressful situations may have caused her to exercise great self-control over a long period of time, and it may be hard to let go and begin to speak, because she is afraid she will come unstuck and release the emotions she has been holding in. And very likely, when the Spirit touches her emotions, that is exactly what will happen. She may begin to weep. This is exactly what she needs to do, so let her weep. If she is being too noisy about it, lay your hand on her head and say quietly, "Take it easy now. Just relax. There's nothing wrong with tears. The Holy Spirit is the world's greatest Therapist, so don't be afraid to let go. If you cry a bucket full, that's what you've been needing to do."

If the person has belonged, or now belongs to, a church that strongly disbelieves in the baptism in the Holy Spirit, and has received much teaching

71

against it, even though she herself has come to accept it, she may still have trouble because of subconscious fears. You may need to take her aside and talk to her about it, and perhaps pray against a spirit of fear and unbelief. You may find some helpful thoughts in chapter ten, on "Questions and Problems."

You may have someone who is very loudly demonstrative. If she is obviously bothering other people, simply go to her, put your hand on her head or shoulder and say, "Take it easy. Relax." She will almost always quiet down immediately.

Someone may begin to laugh. This is great, and not usually any problem. In fact, Holy Spirit-inspired laughter is very infectious, and can really help everyone relax and enjoy the Lord, unless, again, the person is being too noisy or silly. If so, again, tell her gently to calm down a bit, and she will. People usually are not out of control, although on occasion they may look and sound like it.

No matter how carried away people may seem to be by the reality of the Holy Spirit, they are actually in full possession of their faculties, and can control themselves, although they may not feel like doing it. If something strikes you very funny, you may want very much to laugh, but you can control yourself if you have to. If you were at a funeral, you would not laugh, no matter how funny the thing was. If you were, say, in a classroom when something struck you as very amusing, you might burst out laughing, but if the professor said, "Please control yourself, you are disturbing the class," you would be able to comply.

After all, there is nothing abnormal about people getting excited about God. At a football game we would think it strange if someone sat in stony silence (unless the person's team was being utterly wiped out), and God is more exciting than any ball game.

If you feel someone is really getting out of line, speak to him firmly, and if he seems really upset, take him off away from the group and talk with him (or have another trained person do it). Try to find out what is wrong, and then pray about the problem. If the cults and occult have already been dealt with, the person usually needs soul or inner healing, and should be told to seek that before trying to continue in the Spirit. There may, of course, be a need for deliverance, which can be a part of the soul-healing process. (See chapter ten, "Questions and Problems" for further material.)

9

Prayer for the Baptism in the Holy Spirit

[When you feel people are ready, pray something like this:]

Father, I claim the protection of the blood of Jesus over us. I ask You to send your angels to stand around us and drive away any spirit of fear, doubt, or confusion.

Holy Spirit, we ask for a new Pentecost here among Your people. Praise You Lord: Father, Son, and Holy Spirit.

Let's all pray together like this:

Dear Jesus, I receive You as my Baptizer. Please baptize me in the Holy Spirit. Thank You, Jesus. Jesus, I receive. I accept the new language You have given me. Help me to release it.

Now, like a little child beginning to talk, just speak out the first sounds that come to your lips. Don't even listen to yourself, just begin to make sounds. Keep your mind and heart on the Lord. Talk to Him. Offer Him the syllables that come, just like a child. And after you begin to make sounds, keep on going. Try not to talk in English, or any other language you know. You can't speak in two languages at once. Pay no attention to any doubt, just keep on speaking. Don't worry about how you feel or how you sound. Just keep talking to God in the new words He is giving you. You are speaking to your Father in heaven. Tell Him the things you need to say to Him.

[At this point, ask your helpers to come and move around the group, helping and encouraging people to begin to pray in the Spirit.]

It's perfectly all right to sing if you want to. This is what the apostle Paul calls "singing in the Spirit." Some people at first find it easier to begin to sing in the new language than to speak in it. You can sometimes get free in singing when you can't seem to in talking. Let the Holy Spirit guide your words, but also let Him give you a tune. It may begin with a few simple notes, or perhaps it may be a chant on one note. After singing awhile, then try again to speak in the Spirit.

[When the time comes to close the session, have the people all stand and speak in tongues together. It's good to have them sing in the Spirit together, and then stop singing and speak again. You can repeat this procedure once or twice. It really helps some people get more freedom to move back and forth from singing to speaking. If there is no hurry to vacate the building where you are meeting, encourage them to stay and pray as long as they wish.

Tell them to speak on the way home, to speak when they go to bed, and when they wake up in the morning. Encourage them to speak when they are driving the car, or when they are working around the house. Tell them that when they are taking a break at work they should go somewhere they can pray in the Spirit, or if they can't get away from their work, to quietly pray in the Spirit while they are on the job, perhaps while looking through the files. Remind them to pray for others in tongues, and to pray in tongues whenever they have special needs.

Don't forget to encourage the people who have prayed to prepare themselves to pray with others, so that renewal in the Holy Spirit will continue to move through the world.]

10

QUESTIONS AND PROBLEMS

[A chapter addressed to you.]

The more people get questions answered, the more easily they will receive, so let them know their questions are acceptable. Don't let the question period get too long, of course, and be sure to stay on the subject of the baptism with the Holy Spirit. Here are some things you may be asked.

DO I HAVE TO SPEAK IN TONGUES?

Some people will say, "You don't *have* to speak in tongues when you are baptized in the Spirit. It's only one of the gifts, after all. Some people get one gift and some another. You may get the gift of tongues, or you may get prophecy, or healing, or something else."

This, of course, means they haven't grasped the difference between the gift of tongues and the prayer language. We went over this in chapter three, so if they are really stuck at this point you may want to suggest that they read chapter three out of this book for themselves, and also read *The Holy Spirit and You.*

STOPPING SHORT

Someone may say, "I prayed for the baptism in the Holy Spirit and I know I received it. I didn't speak in tongues, but I just really felt wonderful."

What does that mean? Did that person receive the baptism with the Holy Spirit? Well, remember, if he's accepted Jesus, the Holy Spirit is living in him, and when he prayed, the Spirit was stirred within him, and he became more aware of Him. Praise the Lord. But if he stopped at that point, as many do, saying, "I must have been baptized in the Spirit because I really felt His presence" or "because I have a new interest in the Scriptures" or "because I have a new desire to tell others" but does not go on to speak in tongues, he is still not at the level of freedom and awareness where God wants him, and he will probably not keep the freedom he has received. He has not yet fully released the Spirit. In order to do that he must be willing to allow the Lord to direct his voice.

People will try to substitute other experiences for speaking in tongues. This in itself is proof that it is important for us to release our voices to God. We don't want to, because the voice is our chief means of expression and therefore the last outpost of our independence. To allow someone else, even God Himself, to guide our voices is a profound act of submission. Therefore we resist it, and want something else in its place.

Imagine Peter saying, on the Day of Pentecost, "I don't need to speak in tongues. After all, I've walked on water."

For example, some people have seen visions, some have had profound experiences of healing. Someone else, when he feels the touch of the Spirit, is moved to copious tears. This is certainly a manifestation of the Spirit, just as *holy laughter* is. Again, every Christian is indwelt by the Holy Spirit, and the sign of that indwelling may be tears, laughter, healings, or miracles, but he or she still needs to speak in tongues in order to receive the blessings that it brings. It performs a special function. *It is not an optional "gift" among many.* So don't try to substitute something else, however wonderful it may be, for speaking in tongues.

81

Cults and Occult

You are likely to get further questions about renouncing the cults and the occult. Someone may remind you of an example you did not mention, or you may be challenged on something you have said. The person may say, "I don't see anything wrong with Christian Science. My grandmother is a devout Christian Scientist." or "My business partner is a Mormon, and he is a clean-living man with high standards; why are you picking on his religion?"

If this happens, don't argue. If you see the person is not himself involved in the cult, but just doesn't understand why you seem to be intolerant of someone else's religion, you may say, "There isn't time to explain it in detail right now, but if you will talk to me after the meeting I will recommend some books for you to read, so that you can help your business partner (or your grandmother) understand, too."

On the other hand, if you see that the person is himself in the cult, or has been in the cult, and is not willing to admit it is wrong, say to him or her, "I understand your feelings, and please forgive me if I have offended you. But I ask you for your own sake not to pray for the baptism with the Holy Spirit until you understand what I am trying to say. If you will stay after the meeting I will recommend some books for you to read."

WHY SO COMPLICATED?

Someone may say, "Why does it have to be so complicated? In the Bible they just received the Spirit and began to speak. They didn't need a long explanation of what they were supposed to do, and they didn't have to be told how to speak in tongues."

Your answer may be something like this: "The people we read about in the New Testament had not been taught it was wrong to express their feelings, so they responded easily and naturally to the prompting of the Holy Spirit. Most of us have been told from childhood that we must not show our emotions, besides which we have been brought up in a culture that refers everything to the intellect, and wants to know "why?" That's why we have to deal with questions, and explanations, and why we have to urge people to open their mouths and begin to speak."

In Acts 10 you can read how Cornelius, the Roman army officer, and his friends began to speak in tongues spontaneously. On the other hand, in Acts 8 Peter and John had to lay their hands on the Samaritan people before they received the Spirit, and Paul did the same in Ephesus in Acts 19:1-7.

"But Jesus didn't speak in tongues, so why do I have to?" Jesus didn't need to speak in tongues, any more than we will need to do so when He returns. "When that which is perfect is come, then that which is in part will be done away" (1 Corinthians 13: 10). Speaking in tongues is for this time in which we are still seeing through glass, dimly *(enigma* is the Greek word Paul uses in First Corinthians 13:12, and it means "a puzzle"). Speaking in tongues is the marvelous ability God gives us to penetrate the dimness and contact Him directly. Jesus needed no such method. He was always in perfect fellowship with the Father. Jesus foretells that we will speak in tongues, in Mark 16:17b. (Some will tell you that this is from the lost ending of Mark, but it certainly comes to us from the early days, and reflects the beliefs of the earliest Christians.)

HYPNOTISM

People often ask whether hypnotism is a cult. The answer depends on what is meant by hypnotism. The *Encyclopedia Britannica* defines hypnotism as: "A sleep-like state during which hallucinatory experiences, distortions in memory, and a wide range of behavioral responses may be induced through suggestion." *Webster's Dictionary* defines it: "A state that resembles sleep but is induced by a hypnotizer whose suggestions are readily accepted by the subject." This is what people usually mean when they refer to hypnotism.

On the other hand, some will use the term hypnotism for any narrowing of the attention brought about through suggestion. This would mean that any attempt to control your own or someone else's behavior by suggestion would be hypnotic. Just telling a friend to cheer up when he is feeling blue would be considered a mild form of hypnotism, but obviously it wouldn't be an occult activity. But almost always, when people ask about hypnotism they mean someone being put into an unconscious state in which he or she will act on suggestions from the hypnotizer.

Clearly you can't flatly say all hypnotism is occult. We don't believe it is a good practice, but the doctor or dentist who uses hypnotism with a patient who cannot take anesthetic is not trying to use some occult power. On the other hand, using hypnotism supposedly to regress a person back to a previous lifetime is an occult practice, and this illustrates the problem very well.

If the hypnotist does try to discover a supposed previous existence, the subject may very likely come up with seeming memories about having lived before, and sometimes the times, places, events, etc., in those memories are found to be accurate. How can this happen? Simple enough. The person is in a trance, open to suggestion from the hypnotizer, but also open to suggestion from spirits in the psychic world, who are only too ready to provide information as it is requested, just as these same spirits will deceive people attending a seance. They are the ones who plant the seeming memories of former existences in the hypnotized person's mind to be discovered by the hypnotist.

This is the danger of hypnotism. Even though the person doing the hypnotizing does not mean to do any harm, and has no occult intention, wherever the human mind is made passive, the enemy is ready to take advantage.

Various results can follow. A person can undergo a total change in personality through being hypnotized. I have known of people becoming depressed, and I have known of a strong Christian leader who went off into strange doctrines after getting involved with hypnotism.

I have known persons unable to speak in tongues until they had renounced the effects of hypnotism.

I strongly recommend to people that they neither allow themselves to be hypnotized, nor attempt to hypnotize others. Although I sympathize with them in their dilemma, I have to discourage people who are unable to take normal anesthesia from allowing themselves to be hypnotized for medical or dental reasons, because even innocent episodes of hypnotism can open the door to problems. Again, this doesn't mean the dentist or doctor intends anything wrong, but that the enemy is ready to take advantage of a passive mind, and provide his own suggestions on the side, so to speak. If the doctor is a believer, and especially if he or she is baptized in the Holy Spirit, the patient should discuss the problem very frankly with him or her.

I would say, "If you have been hypnotized, even for innocent purposes, recognize that something may have gained access to your mind which needs to be cast out. Say, 'Lord, I'm sorry I allowed myself to be hypnotized. Please forgive me. I accept Your forgiveness. If anything wrong came into my soul while I was hypnotized, I renounce it, bind it, and cast it out, and any spirits associated with it, in Jesus' Name, under His precious blood.'"

If this explanation does not satisfy the inquirer, and he is not willing to renounce any wrong influence that may have come through being hypnotized, suggest that he not pray for the baptism with the Holy Spirit until he does understand the dangers of hypnotism and is willing to pray against them.

FRATERNAL ORGANIZATIONS

You may get a question regarding fraternal organizations. There is no doubt that at least one of the leading lodges crosses paths with the occult in its higher degrees, and that its basic theology is not Trinitarian. On the other hand, for many people lodges are simply for socializing, and they would not understand why they are spiritually dangerous. My feeling at present is that you should point out the danger, but leave it to the individuals to do research on the issue themselves. Tell them that if they belong to or have belonged to a fraternal organization, when they join in the prayer of renunciation, they should renounce anything in the teachings of that organization that might be contrary to the Scriptures.

This kind of thing applies to other organizations vows and promises that are given, and ceremonies gone through. Most fraternities and sororities are oriented toward the ancient Greek deities. Did any vows made in your fraternity or sorority invoke the Greek gods or goddesses? If so, they should be renounced. Doctors might take another look at the traditional Hippocratic oath, still used in graduation ceremonies at some medical schools, which is made in the name of Apollo and the other Greek gods and goddesses. The parts of this oath concerned with medical practice certainly do not need to be renounced, in fact certain aspects of it need to be reasserted today (look it up in the encyclopedia), but a Christian doctor who has taken this oath ought to renounce its pagan orientation, and reaffirm its principles in the name of the true God.   Don't dismiss this as silly, saying, "Why that sort of thing is just for fun. I didn't take it seriously." Agnes Sanford tells how as a child in China she went into a Buddhist temple, and just to see what would happen, bowed before the idol and recited the chant she had heard the monks say. Says Agnes, "Nothing happened. Or did it? I wonder. For gradually there came to be within me another voice, sneering, despising, scorning me." And she tells how, many years later, a perceptive friend discerned and cast out the spirit that had attached itself to her when she went through this childish piece of foolishness.

GRAPHOLOGY

I am often asked about graphology, or handwriting analysis. If graphology teaches simply that a person's handwriting reflects his mood or personality makeup, and that studying his handwriting may be useful to help him understand himself, rather obviously this would not be occult.

But if graphology is being used like palmistry to read a person's future, it would of course be occult. Since the question quite often comes up, I presume handwriting analysis is sometimes used for this kind of thing. I have never directly encountered it myself.

STRANGE MANIFESTATIONS

I am not here talking about people getting excited and blessed, and perhaps getting a little noisy and disturbing others. I dealt with that in the last chapter. I am concerned here with really weird actions that clearly are not from the Holy Spirit. If you prepare people carefully, and make sure they have accepted the Lord and have renounced any involvement with the occult or the cults, you are not likely to have such manifestations. If, however, someone does begin to behave in a weird or frightening manner, take firm authority in the name of Jesus. If this does not seem to take care of the situation, have experienced counselors gently escort the person away from the group into another room, and try to find out what is troubling him.

Claim God's protection over yourself and everyone present, and then, if the person is rational and cooperative, ask him to name the thing that is troubling him—fear, anger. etc.—and then lead him to pray, "Spirit of fear [or whatever it is] in Jesus' Name, I bind you and cast you out of my life, never to return to this earth, or to trouble any human being again; under the precious blood of Jesus." It is important to have the person pray like this for himself, while you agree with him. There may or may not be any outward sign that anything has happened. People do sometimes cough, sneeze, yawn, cry out, or even vomit when receiving deliverance, but in our experience most do not. This does not mean nothing has happened, though.

The problem may have gotten into the person's life through deep hurts in the soul, so urge him to seek inner healing before trying to continue in the Spirit.

At an Episcopal Church in Virginia many years ago, I had prepared a group of people as thoroughly as I could. There were some forty kneeling around the altar seeking to receive the baptism with the Holy Spirit. (In those days we were still praying individually for people, with laying on of hands. Nowadays, as I have shared in this book, we like to pray with the group first, and then encourage them individually.)

As I went around the altar, I came to a man who, as we prayed, literally began to bang his head on the brass altar rail. It didn't take much discernment to see he had a problem, so I signaled to two friends who were working with me. They took the chap into another area and prayed with him. They found he had been into Swedenborgianism, a spiritualist cult. As he described it to me afterwards, although he had prayed to cast out wrong things from his life, this Swedenborgian spirit was still troubling him, and when he began to release the Holy Spirit, he felt a battle inside him between the Holy Spirit and the Swedenborgian spirit, and that was why he was behaving so strangely. As soon as the wrong spirit was dealt with, this man joyfully received the baptism with the Holy Spirit and was just fine.

In England while I was praying with a group, a young minister fell on the floor and began to yell and writhe. Again I asked two people with me to take him in the next room. They cast two spirits out

91

of him, and then prayed for him to be baptized in the Holy Spirit. When that young clergyman had arrived at the meeting that night, he had looked like "death warmed over." When he left, he was happy and smiling!

If the distressed person seems unable to cooperate, the people praying with him should first claim the protection of the blood of Jesus over themselves and all others around, and then speak directly to the disturbing spirit something like this, "In Jesus' Name, you disturbing spirit [or whatever name they feel led to give it, depending on how the person is behaving], I bind you and cast you out, never to return, or to trouble any human being again, under the precious blood of Jesus, Amen."

If some wrong spirit does slip into the situation, don't be afraid; you have complete authority over it, but do get the person out and away from the rest of the people, and call someone else to deal with them so you can continue to help the others who are praying.

DOES SPEAKING IN TONGUES COME FROM THE UNCONSCIOUS MIND?

You are not too likely to be asked this question when you are instructing, but you should know the answer yourself. Speaking in tongues is not from the subconscious mind. It comes directly from the Holy Spirit.

Who is living in the human spirit of every believing Christian, and it is the indwelling Spirit Who provides the language. For example, a friend of mine spoke fluently in Mandarin at a prayer meeting. This man had no knowledge of Chinese. A Chinese lady who was present (her husband was a physician, on an exchange fellowship at the University of Washington) said, "How can this man speak so fluently in Mandarin? Where did he learn?" "What is he saying?" we asked her. "Oh, he's just praising and glorifying God." she said. Said a skeptic, "He probably was taken to a Chinese restaurant when he was a child, his subconscious mind absorbed the words he heard, and now he's reciting them back."

To this my daughter Margaret gave the obvious answer, "Then he would be reciting the menu, wouldn't he?"

Some teach that the subconscious mind is the spirit, and that we contact God through the subconscious. The subconscious mind is not the spirit, it is the vast depository for all the memories and feelings of the past. Nor does God come into the human spirit by way of the unconscious. However, His Spirit can plumb the depths of the unconscious and heal the hurts that trouble our conscious lives. Through speaking in tongues the Spirit can give us the words to express and confess material from the unconscious, and so offer it to God for Him to deal with.

93

I Feel It's Just Me Speaking

Someone may say, "I feel I'm forcing what I am saying when I try to speak in tongues—that it's just me speaking. It's such hard work to do it, it can't really be my prayer language."

Many people get stuck at this point, and, as I said, the enemy is only too ready to tell them, "That's not it." or "That's just you."

Tell those people not to believe the enemy, and not to give up trying to speak. Tell them, "Remember what speaking in tongues is. It isn't being taken over by the Holy Spirit and *made* to speak another language. It is you speaking, and trusting the Lord living in you to guide you and give you the words. You are the one making the effort to speak, and at first this may be difficult. But as you try to speak and let the Lord guide you, He can begin to give you what He wants. Really, the very first sound or syllable you utter while trying to trust the Lord is the first syllable of your new language. So keep on speaking while keeping your mind and heart on the Lord.

Try not to listen to yourself. Sometimes it's a good idea to be doing something else while you are trying to pray in the Spirit. Try it while you are driving the car, vacuuming the rugs, taking a shower—when your mind is on some other activity. Don't stop. Keep on with it, and you will get free.

Some people, when they first try to speak in the Spirit, may sound like the chant of an auctioneer. That's all right, tell them to just keep on chanting, but slow down and let the words begin to form. A friend of mind was determined to speak, but he was so tense that all he could get out was a kind of loud groan. But he hung in there. His wife said, laughing, "He was making such a racket I went around and closed all the windows and doors because the neighbors were gathering on the front lawn." But, after two hours, he broke through and began to speak in tongues.

God is not making it difficult. It's just that one of the hardest things for us human beings to do is really let go of our inhibitions.

PSYCHOLOGICAL TONGUES?

For a long time opponents of speaking in tongues liked to say it was "of the devil," and you will find that some still do. It's hard to get away with a statement like that today, though, so now you may hear a different kind of put-down for speaking in tongues. Some are saying, "It's okay—it's not bad, or pathological, and the people who do it are quite normal—however, it's of the natural man and not of the Spirit. It is purely psychological."

You may get a question along this line.

Some will claim that the tongues on the Day of Pentecost were from the Spirit, but the "Corinthian tongues" (1 Corinthians 12-14) were just psychological. They will say that's why Paul supposedly tried to restrict the Corinthians from doing it. As a matter of fact, I have heard a good, sincere pastor maintain that Paul did not speak in tongues at all. When he said he "spoke in tongues more than you all," (1 Corinthians 14:18) he simply meant he was master of nine languages. This is nonsense, of course, but it is a good example of how far people will twist the Scriptures to avoid accepting something that is against their preconceived ideas.

The spirits of the Christians at Corinth were joined to the Lord just as were those of the first believers in the book of Acts. "He that is joined to the Lord is one Spirit" (1 Corinthians 6:17). When a Christian prays in tongues, his human spirit, joined to the Lord, is praying. Whether it's the people at the first Pentecost in Acts 2, or the believers at Corinth, or you and me these days, praying in tongues isn't natural prayer, but supernatural prayer.

It's stated very clearly in the Amplified Bible. "For if I pray in an [unknown] tongue, my spirit [by the Holy Spirit within me] prays . . ." (1 Corinthians 14:14, 15).

Speaking in tongues is not a psychological activity at all, since it does not come from the soul (psyche) but from the spirit. When you speak in tongues, your mind is "unfruitful" as Paul put it (1 Corinthians 14:14b)—i.e., the words you are saying do not come from your mind. The only part the mind plays in speaking in tongues is in directing the use of the voice apparatus itself. When you speak in tongues you are praying from your spirit (1 Corinthians 14:14a).

Deaf-mute people, who have never spoken a word in a natural language (although their speech apparatus is normal) will sometimes speak in tongues when they are baptized in the Holy Spirit. I heard this happen myself, not more than a month ago, and those who work with the deaf testify that it happens. Since a deaf-mute person has no psychological ability to speak, the speaking in tongues must come directly from the spirit to the vocal organs.

A close friend of ours lost his speech for a short time following a mild stroke, but although he could not say a word in human language, he was able to speak in tongues throughout. He was not able to call upon his memories of English, or to operate his vocal mechanism to speak English, but because the language of the Spirit comes directly from the Lord, he had no difficulty in speaking in tongues.

Be very cautious about accepting the results of scientific research in this area. Trying to evaluate spiritual things from the outside, by objective measurements, is like trying to discover what apple pie tastes like by external investigation.

Don't Members of the Cults Speak in Tongues?

Some of the people in the cult religions claim to speak in tongues. What about this?

The cult religions also claim to manifest other spiritual gifts. Some are built around the idea of healing. Others would claim the power to prophesy the future, or to receive mystical wisdom and knowledge. All these manifestations would come from the same source as the supposed speaking in tongues—that is, from the psychic world. The fact that a person supposedly speaks in tongues, or seems to heal the sick, or has knowledge beyond his or her natural ability, does not prove those things are from God. The enemy is a great counterfeiter. If you want to know whether someone is moving in the power of the Holy Spirit, you don't ask them to heal the sick or speak in a strange language, you ask them, "Have you received Jesus as your Savior and Lord?"

Something Bad Said in Tongues?

Now and then someone will say something like, "I heard from a friend of mine that *she* was told by a friend of hers that a missionary was at a meeting somewhere and someone spoke in tongues. The missionary understood the language, and the person was cursing God. How can I be sure I won't do something like that if I speak in a language I can't understand?"

This story has been going around for a long, long, time. It is always said that someone's friend was told by someone else, who heard it from somewhere else, but you will never be able to find out where this supposed event happened.

It is absolutely impossible that any Christian person praying or speaking in the Holy Spirit (in tongues) should say anything bad. How can I be sure? Because, as Paul says, "No one can be speaking under the influence of the Holy Spirit and say, 'Curse Jesus,' and on the other hand, no one can say, 'Jesus is Lord' unless he is under the influence of the Holy Spirit" (1 Corinthians 12:3, JB).

If someone asks this question, tell him:

"If you have received the Lord Jesus, and therefore the Holy Spirit is living in your spirit, anything that you speak from your spirit is going to be from the Lord. Jesus said that if we ask God for a fish, He isn't going to give us a snake, and if we ask for an egg, we're not going to be given a scorpion. If we ask for bread, we're not going to get a rock. (Luke 11:11-13). So if you, trusting God, speak the words that come to your lips, they're not going to be bad words.

"Of course, it is possible that someone in a public meeting who is not a Christian, might be controlled by a demonic spirit, and bring a false manifestation. That is the only way the missionary story could be true. But that is nothing that should worry you. You are not controlled by a wrong spirit, but indwelt by the Holy Spirit."

WHAT AGE CAN CHILDREN BE BAPTIZED IN THE SPIRIT?

You may have young children in the group you are instructing, or you may be asked this question by a parent.

Some say that Jesus will not baptize a child in the Spirit, because a child is not ready to minister. And you don't need the baptism, they would say, until you are ready to minister, that is, do something to serve God.

I believe this is exactly backwards. You don't get baptized in the Spirit because you are ready to minister, you want to minister *because you* have been baptized in the Spirit. It is the baptism in the Holy Spirit that *makes* people willing and able to minister, and that goes for children and adults both.

A girl in my former parish received the baptism in the Holy Spirit at the age of four-and-a-half. Shortly after, she insisted on laying hands on another child whose wrist was injured, and he was immediately healed.

The six-year-old daughter of the senior warden of an Episcopal Cathedral on the East Coast was baptized in the Holy Spirit (both her parents were charismatic Christians). While Rita and I were at that church, this youngster came to Rita, bringing a five-year-old friend, and asked Rita to help her lead her friend to Jesus. The baptism in the Spirit is not given *for* ministry, rather it *results* in ministry, in child or adult.

There is no way to set an age limit on receiving the baptism in the Holy Spirit. In all seriousness, I suspect there are those who spoke in tongues in their infancy before they spoke their native language. The son of an Episcopal priest, an acquaintance of mine, received the baptism in the Holy Spirit and spoke in tongues at the age of two-and-a-half. The youngster had a bad cold, and the father laid hands on him to pray for healing, when to the father's surprise the boy began to speak fluently in tongues. As the child grew up, it was evident that he had indeed received the freedom of the Spirit.

As far as ministering is concerned, one of the unhappy teachings of the older Pentecostal movement was that the baptism in the Holy Spirit was given for *service*. This was probably said in self-protection, because other Christians accused the Pentecostals of enjoying their faith a little too much. They were not being serious about it. All this is such a sad mistake. God wants all His people—big and little, old and young—to receive the freedom of the Holy Spirit, just as soon as they desire it, not primarily because He wants them to serve Him, but because He wants them to know how wonderful He is. We need not be afraid to claim that the *first* purpose of the baptism in the Spirit is simply *joy,* pleasure in the Lord's presence, dancing, singing, clapping hands. Burdens lifted. Healing. Blessing. After that, it is the most natural thing in the world to *want* to share this with others. Until they are taught to be "serious," it's difficult to *stop* people from spreading their joy around after they have been baptized in the Holy Spirit.

We find many people who remember having spoken in tongues in childhood without knowing what it was. "I remember as a young child running over the lawn, happily speaking in this other language," said one Anglican priest we know. One night at a meeting in California, two rather proper-looking older ladies (I believe they were Lutheran) attended instruction to receive the Holy Spirit. They were obviously nervous about the whole thing, so I took them aside and talked with them. As we chatted, one of them said suddenly, "Father Bennett, could this be something I did when I was a child?"

"Yes," I said, "that's quite possible."

It turned out she had indeed prayed in the Spirit when she was a small child, and before the session was over, she and I laid hands on the other lady, and she too received the baptism in the Spirit.

Children will sometimes begin to speak in tongues as they hear their parents doing so in family prayer. In the early days of the renewal, it was not unusual to have whole families receive the baptism in the Spirit—grandparents, parents, children, and grandchildren.

No one can say for sure when a person is or isn't ready for the freedom of the Spirit. Do not, of course, pressure a young child to receive, any more than you would pressure an adult, but if a child is interested, answer his questions, and let the initiative come from him.

All this, of course, assumes that parents are involved. You should not, under normal circumstances, pray with a child to receive the baptism in the Holy Spirit without the parent's consent and support. This goes for teenagers, too.

Not only would you be violating parental authority, you may also make it very difficult for a child or young person if he has been opened to life in the Spirit, and yet does not get continued support, teaching and fellowship, to say nothing of perhaps meeting active opposition at home.

Remember, this is talking about the baptism in the Holy Spirit. It doesn't apply to leading a child to receive Jesus as Savior. I don't think you should ever hesitate to do that under any circumstances.

If children are in the group you are instructing, they will almost certainly be with a parent, so you need not hesitate to work with them. Sometimes parents will have the child there when the child isn't really ready, or doesn't understand, and you should be sensitive to that. (Note the last topic in this list of questions and problems.) Do not in any way cajole or pressure the youngster. If he or she is obviously not ready, just ask God to bless him or her, and leave it in His hands.

"I Dreamed I Was Speaking in Tongues"

It is not unusual for someone, perhaps after asking for the baptism in the Holy Spirit and trying unsuccessfully to pray in the Spirit, to *dream* he is speaking in tongues. If someone tells you this has happened to him, tell him it's great, and reassure him or her that he or she was indeed praying in the

Spirit in the dream. This seems to be one of the ways in which the Lord can get past our inhibitions.

It is important to follow this up, and to point out to the person that he can do the same thing in his waking life, and encourage him to try it. He will usually find he can do it easily.

OTHER VARIETIES OF SPEAKING IN TONGUES

The Lord seems to have many methods of doing things. Remember how many different ways He would go about healing people? Sometimes He would put His hands on them, sometimes He would just speak a word of command, and a healing would take place, perhaps at a distance. He healed by putting mud on a blind man's eyes. A number of times people were healed just by touching His clothing.

It isn't surprising then that speaking in tongues comes in variety, too. One man, while praying for the baptism in the Spirit, began to see words moving across his mind's eye like a ticker tape. Another saw the words as if printed on the wall. If something like this happens just say, "Read 'em off."

People will sometimes say, "I've got these silly syllables in my mind, but they couldn't be right." Tell them to speak them out.

You never know what a tongue is going to sound like. I had an acquaintance who sounded like "rub-a-dubdub" when he spoke in tongues, but he got a great blessing out of doing it. He was kind of a slow old stick, and I thought, "Well, he isn't too quick on the intake. He probably isn't getting it right. What he's saying couldn't really be a language, but he's getting a blessing, so I'm not going to question it."

The next week I was in the international sector of Seattle and heard two oriental gentlemen conversing on a street corner. As I caught their words, it sounded like "rub-a-dub-dub," just exactly as my friend had sounded when he was speaking in tongues. I said, "Excuse me, Lord, for jumping to conclusions.

Years ago, at a meeting in Walla Walla, Washington, an elderly lady began to speak in tongues—that is to say, she began to make clicking noises with her tongue. As she clicked she began to get happy in the Spirit, and when she left that night she was still clicking, her face shining with joy. I might have been disturbed by this had not a missionary friend recently told me of the "click" languages of Southern Africa, spoken by Bushmen and the Khoisan people. I can't prove, of course, that the lady was speaking in Khoikhoin, but whatever it was, it certainly made her happy.

WHY DO MISSIONARIES HAVE TO LEARN LANGUAGES?

If it is possible for God to give people languages instantly by the Holy Spirit, why then do missionaries have to spend time in language school, preparing to go to another country? Why can't they just receive the language from the Lord directly?

This is a question you'll sometimes be asked, and it puzzles people who don't understand the usual nature and purpose of speaking in tongues. A lot of this confusion arises from a false picture of Pentecost itself. It's surprising how many informed Christians think the other languages spoken at Pentecost were in order to proclaim the Gospel in those languages to the people listening because they were from "every nation under heaven" (Acts 2:5). In other words, Pentecost was a missionary activity. But what the passage actually says is that there were dwelling at Jerusalem "Jews, devout men, out of every nation under heaven."

With the exception of a few "proselytes" from Rome, people who had converted to Judaism, the people in Jerusalem at Pentecost were not Gentiles or foreigners. They were simply Jewish people who lived in other countries, and who had come back to Jerusalem for the feast. They did not need to be spoken to in foreign languages. What they heard was not a proclamation of the Gospel, but they heard these first Christians praising and glorifying God for the wonderful things He had done (verse 11).

When Peter began to speak to them to explain what was happening, he did proclaim the Gospel, but he didn't do it in a foreign language. And he didn't call them "Gentiles and foreigners," but "men and brethren" (verse 29).

The people were impressed by the other languages because they were the tongues of the various countries where they lived. The Jews from Rome didn't need to be spoken to in Latin, but they were amazed to hear Galilean fishermen speaking in perfect Latin.

Remember the first purpose of speaking in tongues is praying in the Spirit to the Lord in a language no man understands. The next use of tongues is to bring a message to a group of people by means of interpretation of tongues. When this happens, occasionally the tongue will be one that is familiar to someone present. When it is interpreted by a gift of the Holy Spirit by someone who does not know the language, the interpretation will be found to match the natural translation of the language, which of course builds up faith.

I remember one of the first Full Gospel Business Men's meetings I attended, many years ago. The leader asked for prayer for his little grandson.

Someone spoke in tongues, and there was an interpretation giving assurance that the child was being healed. Later I found that an acquaintance of mine, who was fluent in the French language, had understood the tongue. The person speaking in tongues had spoken in French, but he did not know French. He was speaking in the Spirit. The person who interpreted the tongue did not know French— he interpreted in the Spirit. But the man who knew French said that the natural translation of the speaking, and the interpretation brought by the Spirit, agreed perfectly.

Also there is a variety of the gift of tongues in which the person will speak in a language he does not know, for a particular purpose, usually to communicate with someone. A member of my own congregation, Amy Stoller, used to go down to the county hospital regularly, looking for people in need of help and encouragement. One day she found a little man sitting on the edge of his bed looking very sad. "May I pray with you?" she asked.

He replied sadly and brokenly, "I no speak English." Said Amy, "I just knew I was supposed to talk to him, so I just began to speak in tongues." The man brightened up, and said, excitedly, that he knew what she was saying because she was speaking in "Canary Islands' Spanish." The two prayed together, and my friend said, "I prayed every word with him in his own language."

109

There are many stories confirming this kind of thing. A mutual friend, a doctor, led a Jewish woman to Jesus by speaking to her in perfect Hebrew, saying, "Daughter of Zion, turn your eyes on Jesus." Which she did. The doctor did not know Hebrew.

The list could go on and on. A missionary was saved from cannibals by speaking to them in their own language. This happened to H.B. Garlock, while a missionary in Africa. The story is told in the little book, *Before We Kill and Eat You,* published by *Christ for the Nations* in Dallas, Texas, in 1974. A friend of ours, Dr, Costa Deir, tells how he made his way through immigration in another country by speaking to the official in tongues. He doesn't know to this day what he said, or in what language, but they let him through!

But in all these cases, the person did not understand the language he was speaking. He just accepted the words as the Lord gave them and trusted they were right for the occasion. Examples of people receiving the permanent ability to speak another language and understand it are few and far between. St. Francis Xavier, the famed missionary to China, is reported to have received the ability to speak the Chinese language miraculously. I have never known anyone to receive a complete language in this way, although I have heard indirect reports of it, and believe it to be possible. I have encountered people who received a greater facility in a language they already partly knew.

An acquaintance of mine, pastor of a neighboring church, hearing about the baptism in the Holy Spirit, asked me to come and talk with him about it. He said, "I was brought up in the Philippines, and I still remember something of the dialect I spoke as a child. I'd like to try to pray in that dialect."

He accordingly bowed his head and began to speak. After a few moments he looked up in surprise. "I don't know the language that well," he said, "I'm not that fluent."

On another occasion a young Jewish Christian prayed for the baptism in the Holy Spirit and began to speak in Arabic. Said he, "That's Arabic, and I know a little Arabic, but I don't know that much." If God could increase a person's knowledge of a language in that way, certainly He could give the whole language.

Presumably the introduction of an entire language into the human memory is a far greater miracle than a person accepting a language word by word to meet a time of need. Nothing is impossible with God, but again our human inability to receive is limited.

We are only at the beginning of this great renewal in the Holy Spirit, and we may see this miracle happening as the years go by. Praise the Lord!

Still, we are called to be fellow workers with God, and perhaps it is not quite in keeping with His style to automatically endow us with a language when we have the time and ability to learn it for ourselves. Perhaps this might come a little too close to manipulating us for God's liking. He values our free will so highly.

"I Was Pressured to Speak in Tongues"

You may occasionally have someone who was really pressured to speak in tongues. Here is a young woman whose mother was so anxious for her teen-age daughter to receive the baptism in the Holy Spirit that she virtually besieged her with a well-meaning group of prayer warriors one day, and in order to escape from their efforts on her behalf, the daughter stammered out a few words and then burst from the room, weeping in humiliation and anger.

The mother and the friends assumed these were tears of blessing, but they weren't. The result was that the girl did not continue to pray in the Spirit, and developed a thorough dislike for the whole operation. Yet she was hungry for more of God. How do you deal with a situation like this?

112

If you encounter such a person, obviously you are going to avoid every possible move that she consent to every action taken on her behalf. It is likely she will need to receive inner healing from her past experience. She needs to see Jesus with her as she recalls the ordeal, allowing Him to make the event what He wanted it to be. She needs to forgive those who prayed with her, not just as an adult, but as a bitterly embarrassed youngster.

11

WHAT NEXT?

You have received the Holy Spirit and spoken in tongues tonight. Some of you know for sure, but perhaps some of you still doubt because you didn't feel anything. The enemy will take advantage of this to try to convince you nothing happened. Pay no attention. Keep on praying in the Spirit as often as you can. If you have doubts, just decide to trust God that it is real. Declare a moratorium on doubt for at least two weeks. Each day thank God for baptizing you in the Spirit, praise Him in your new language, and at the end of the time see if there is not some significant change in your life.

Pray often in tongues for your family and friends and about your own needs. You will learn by experience how effective it is.

You need fellowship with other people who are baptized in the Spirit. Do not leave your own church. That is where God has put you to spread the Word, but if you cannot get spiritual food there, you will need to find it somewhere else. That doesn't mean, though, that you have to go and join another church. Go to your church on Sunday morning, and then on Sunday night or during the week, go where your spirit can be renewed and fed. The most joyful prayer meeting in your area may be at the local Assembly of God, at the Episcopal Church, the Roman Catholic Church, or with another denomination. If you find a place to go for refreshment of your spirit, by all means go, even though the setting is quite different from what you are used to. Do remember, though, that you are there to share in prayer and praise, not to be hassled about your or their church's teachings, or to be persuaded to leave your church, and join theirs, or to be re-baptized, or something like that. If you do get pressured, just smile and say, "I feel called to stay in my own church, and I hope you can accept me as I am."

Of course, there are times when it is impossible to remain: if your spiritual life is really suffering; if all the doors are closed, and no one is listening to you; if the teachings of the church are clearly wrong and perhaps even demonic; and especially if you have children and there is no sound training for them, or perhaps very unsound training. I heard of one church where the children were encouraged to bring their Ouija boards to Sunday school. In such a case you would have to move. Even then you should be careful where and how you move. Do not leave in anger, but in love and forgiveness. Do not immediately reject your own background and tradition, but go to the nearest church of your own denomination, or of some similar denomination, where you feel you will find satisfactory leadership and teaching. Don't forget, God is trying to reach people in all the churches today, and you may be one of those He is counting on to reach your own group, so don't act in any way that will cause you to lose your impact on people of your own tradition. (If you are married, you and your mate will, of course, need to arrive at a common decision on all this.)

You also need to be in a small fellowship. Find one that is free in the Spirit, where people meet just to have a happy time in the Lord, while remaining active in their respective churches. Be wary, however, of groups made up of free-lancers who have left their churches and are trying to function on their own. These can easily be deceived by some wandering prophet or strange doctrine.

Become familiar with the Scriptures—you will find they have come alive to you in a new way. Be discriminating, though, about Bible studies. If you don't find enough Scripture study available in your own church to meet your need, you may decide to start listening to Bible teachers on the radio or via tape recording, or join a fellowship for Bible study. Unfortunately, some of these teachers and study fellowships are antagonistic to the baptism with the Holy Spirit, so when they talk about the gifts of the Spirit, they will tell you "these things are not for today," and you may even be informed that your experience is from the devil. Such teachers are likely to be strongly legalistic and negative, will not uplift or free your spirit, and may put you under oppression and condemnation.

At the risk of sounding narrow, I will say as a general rule you should not follow any present-day Bible teacher unless he or she is baptized in the Spirit, and testifies openly to his or her experience.

Remember, Bible study should inspire you, and give you spiritual nourishment, not send you on a head trip or confuse you with clever theories.

Read good books about life in the Spirit. Listen to good tapes. Go to good conferences. Again, try to stay with your own church and background if you possibly can, for that is where you will be most effective.

God bless you.

[Encourage people again to continue to pray in the Spirit. If you are able to do so, it would be great to get this same group together after a few days and pray with them again. The more you can keep in touch with them, the better. In any case, suggest that each of them read *The Holy Spirit* and You and if possible have a follow-up class using this book and its study supplement. This will help people understand about the gifts of the Spirit, and how to walk in the Spirit.]

APPENDIX 1

A LISTING OF SOME OTHER RELIGIONS AND PHILOSOPHIES (CULTS)

OLD PAGAN RELIGIONS

Hinduism, Buddhism, Shintoism, Taoism, Islam (Mohammedans, Moslems, or Muslims), Zoroastrianism.

ETHNIC RELIGIONS

American Indian (Medicine Men), Hawaiian (Kahunas), Eskimo (Shamans), Druidism (Celtic religion) and so forth.

MODERN REVIVALS OF PAGANISM

Transcendental Meditation (Hinduism), Black Muslims (Islam), various kinds of Yoga (Hinduism), certain aspects of the Martial Arts (Buddhism), modern interest in Zen and other forms of Buddhism and Hinduism. Modern interest in the ethnic religions.

121

New Religions (made up in relatively recent times)

Latter-day Saints (Mormons), Jehovah's Witnesses
(Russelites), the Mind Science group of religions—
Christian Science, Science of Mind, Unity School of
Christianity, Religious Science. Theosophy. Spiritism or
Spiritualism. Swedenborgianism. Bahai. Soka Gakkai.
(Do not confuse Unitarianism with Unity. Unitarianism
today is usually a humanistic philosophy that does not
claim to be a religion as such.)

There are, of course, many others.

APPENDIX 2

A LIST OF OCCULT PRACTICES

ASTRAL PROJECTION

Trying to achieve out-of-the-body experiences.

ASTROLOGY

Believing that the planets, sun, moon, stars, influence human destiny. Casting horoscopes or getting a horoscope cast. Following zodiacal signs.

AUTOMATIC WRITING

Attempting to get messages from the psychic world by allowing a spirit to guide the hand in writing.

CHARMS

Using a lucky charm of some kind. Amulets. Talismans.

CLAIRVOYANCE

Trying to receive information by second sight.

DRUGS

Using mind altering drugs such as marijuana, LSD, etc.

ESP

Trying to exercise extrasensory perception.

FORTUNE-TELLING OR PRECOGNITION

Attempting to look into the future. Fortune-telling by crystal ball, Tarot cards, cards, reading palms, reading tea-leaves, or using a Ouija board, pendulum, or any other fortune-telling device. Going to a fortune-teller.

MIND CONTROL

Telekinesis, psychokinesis. Attempts to use the power of mind-over-matter. Trying to influence another person by mind control. Trying to project one's thoughts into material things or into other people.

PSYCHIC HEALING

Seeking healing from a person who claims to heal by spiritual power other than through Jesus Christ. Seeking healing through spirit-mediums or psychic healers.

REINCARNATION

Believing one has lived other lives in other bodies. Attempting through hypnosis, etc., to recall those supposed previous lives.

SPIRITISM OR SPIRITUALISM

Attempting to contact disembodied spirits or the psychic world through seances or other methods. Table tapping, or table tilting. Levitation.

TELEPATHY

Mind reading. Trying to read someone else's mind, or project one's thoughts to someone else.

WATER DIVINING OR WATER WITCHING

Attempting to find water, or other things, by use of a divining rod.

WITCHCRAFT, SORCERY, MAGIC

Having anything to do with casting spells, voodoo, or hexing. Making a pact with Satan to get psychic power. Actual worship of Satan (Satanism). Witches' Sabbath. Black mass.

If you have read books telling about the occult out of curiosity you should renounce and destroy them. Any kind of pornography, although not directly occult, opens the way to the occult, and should be renounced. Stage magic is dangerous, too, as although it is known to be trickery, it opens the imagination to the possibility of witchcraft and sorcery.

Available at your local Christian bookstore

Bridge-Logos *Publishers*

1-800-631-5802 http://www.bridgelogos.com